Hellenic Studies 61

THE WEB OF ATHENAEUS

Recent Titles in the Hellenic Studies Series

http://chs.harvard.edu/chs/publications

THE WEB OF ATHENAEUS

Christian Jacob

Translated by
Arietta Papaconstantinou

Edited by
Scott Fitzgerald Johnson

CENTER FOR HELLENIC STUDIES
Trustees for Harvard University
Washington, D.C.
Distributed by Harvard University Press
Cambridge, Massachusetts, and London, England
2013

The Web of Athenaeus by Christian Jacob
Translated by Arietta Papaconstantinou
Edited by Scott Fitzgerald Johnson
Copyright © 2013 Center for Hellenic Studies, Trustees for Harvard University
All Rights Reserved.
Published by Center for Hellenic Studies, Trustees for Harvard University,
    Washington, D.C.
Distributed by Harvard University Press, Cambridge, Massachusetts, and
    London, England
Production: Kristin Murphy Romano
Cover design and illustration: Joni Godlove
Printed by Edwards Brothers, Inc., Ann Arbor, MI

Cataloging-in-Publication Data available from the Library of Congress.
ISBN: 9780674073289

Contents

Contents

Foreword

WHY SHOULD ANYONE bother reading Athenaeus today? Among the extant corpus of Greek texts, the *Deipnosophists* is a paradoxical work, such a long and undigested text, with a confusing structure, a text mainly composed of fragments of other texts, of quotations from a lost a library. Athenaeus, like some other polymaths, scholiasts, or lexicographers, is one of those archivists and transmitters of ancient scholarship, providing contemporary readers with an inexhaustible quarry of data, information, words, citations, *curiosa* and various antiquarian oddities. This quarry is an inevitable starting point for anyone willing to edit the extant fragments of lost works (for example, the poets of Middle Comedy or the Greek historians) or for ballasting the footnotes of modern scholarly texts with thousand of references, pertaining to the widest range of topics one could imagine.

So why should anyone bother reading Athenaeus today, that is, considering his work as a coherent text, as the result from a meaningful project, as related to specific intellectual and literate interests and techniques, as a literary composition worthy of being read?

The shift from using Athenaeus as a mine of pithy references to reading his text in its continuity and architecture provides us with a different standpoint and opens many new perspectives. Instead of focusing on some tiny islands, such as a word, an object or a quotation, one has to take in account a wider horizon. One has to face the width, the extent of an ocean. The 15 books of the *Deipnosophists* are indeed a textual, a scholarly, an antiquarian ocean, and the reader feels disorientated, lost, and puzzled by such a vast and unknown space whose mapping and survey seem out of reach. Trying to understand the reasons of such a disorientation, trying to set up stable landmarks in this textual flood, shedding light on the underlying structure, such would be the only ways for our reader to navigate safely through this text, from the beginning of Book One to the end of Book Fifteen. The purpose of this book is to provide the reader with a map and a compass before he or she enters the world of Athenaeus.

My *periplous* through Athenaeus started in 1996, when I answered a call for papers launched by David Braund and John Wilkins, organizers of the Exeter conference on Athenaeus (1997). I proposed a paper about bibliographical knowledge in the *Deipnosophists*, about Athenaeus as a librarian. A first survey of Athenaeus' text put made me aware of the many links with Alexandrian scholarship and with the history of ancient libraries. Athenaeus and his characters were interested not only in texts and words, but also in books, in their form, in their identification, in their collection.

Athenaeus opened new and unexpected perspectives in my ongoing reflection on ancient libraries, on the Museum of Alexandria and its scholars. My first impression was that the *Deipnosophists* allowed us to observe ancient readers at work and at play. For documenting this hypothesis, I followed a double method. First, I started a full reading of the *Deipnosophists*, from beginning to end, creating an index linking together key words, personal comments, Greek text, and translation. It seemed appropriate and to a certain extent ironic to apply to Athenaeus' text his own method of excerpting, to submit his text to the grid of an intensive and close reading, even when he seemed more interested in expansive reading crossing hundreds of books. Second, I started systematic searches through the *Thesaurus Linguae Graecae* database, in order to gather all the occurrences and the context of keywords such as *biblion, grapsai, pinax, anagignōskein*, etc.

The Exeter Conference proceedings were published in 2000. The book *Athenaeus and His World, Reading Greek Culture in the Roman World* (David Braund and John Wilkins ed., Exeter: University of Exeter Press) was a groundbreaking landmark among studies of Athenaeus and it shed a new light on the text and its context, on the author and his methods, on his library and the ways he used it. This collective endeavor allowed different disciplinary approaches to map the interests of Athenaeus, his use of sources, his connection to learned traditions, either philosophical, medical, grammatical or historiographical.

By that time, I was involved in a new project, far more ambitious. Luciano Canfora invited me to join a team of Italian scholars, coordinated by Leo Citelli and Maria Luisa Gambato, who were working on an annotated translation of the *Deipnosophists*. This new translation was published in 2001, as a set of four luxurious volumes, *Ateneo, I Deipnosofisti, I Dotti a Banchetto* (Rome: Salerno Editrice). I was asked to write the general introduction to these volumes.

Athenaeus and His World was a collective endeavor, bringing together specialists in all the different topics and literary genres Athenaeus was interested in. The purpose of the Exeter conference and volume was to map the *terra incognita* of the *Deipnosophists*, through a thematic coverage, a large scale survey. My essay "Ateneo o il Dedalo delle Parole" ("Athenaeus, or the Labyrinth of Words") tried to draw a small-scale map of the *Deipnosophists*, that is, to face general questions about the nature and the meaning of this text, and the intentions of its author.

The Web of Athenaeus is the English revised version of "Ateneo o il Dedalo delle Parole." My goal is to offer a general introduction to the *Deipnosophists* but also a strong reading hypothesis: beyond the heterogeneous surface of the text, beyond the excesses, the fun, the parody, and the comedy, there is a project, an intent, a scholarly base. Athenaeus himself remains a mysterious author, and we have no biographical information beyond the very few pieces he reveals about himself. His monumental work remains an enigma too. Was it intended for public circulation? For which readers? Was it a tribute to Larensius, the Roman patron of the deipnosophists? Or should we consider that the fifteen books put together by Athenaeus were devoted to his own personal use? We have very little evidence about ancient use of the *Deipnosophists*, but the text survived its author and was known at least, perhaps already in an epitomized form, by Macrobius, Stephanus Byzantinus, Constantinus Porphyrogenitus, the *Suda*, and Eusthatius.

My point in this essay is to understand Athenaeus' intellectual project and also the literary frame he chose, that is, banquet-conversation. It is indeed a traditional genre, already exemplified by Plato, Xenophon, Plutarch, and Petronius. The question is: did Athenaeus use this frame as a mere literary fiction, in order to rearrange hundreds of reading notes, words, and excerpts? Or does the dialogue of Larensius' guests mirror something else, some scholarly and literate interactions in a learned salon at the beginning of the 3rd century AD?

I tried to go deeply into this hypothesis. That is, I consider one should take seriously the characters staged in this banquet, their interactions, the dynamics of their dialogue, the way they comment on their conversation and on their knowledge. As with the *Attic Nights* of Aulus Gellius, Plutarch's *Sumposiaca*, the recently discovered treatise of Galen, *Peri Alupias* (*On the Absence of Grief*), I consider the *Deipnosophists* a field for an anthropologist of ancient knowledge and scholarship. Through this text, its narrative set-up, the dynamics of interaction, and its uninterrupted flow of words, quotations, comments, questions, and answers, one can observe the behavior, the mental mechanisms, the cultural concerns, the scholarly techniques of a group of ancient philosophers, grammarians, jurists, musicians, and physicians at play. The dinner and the symposion were the place of a codified social ritual, they were also a frame for scholarly and intellectual activities, as the Aristotelian school and the Museum of Alexandria testify.

This ritual, these activities are the focus of Athenaeus' attention. His whole work is ruled by reflection and mirrors. The text mirrors the banquet, the talks of Larensius' guests mirror all the dishes, objects, and events of the banquet, Athenaeus articulates in a continuous thread the lively exchanges of his characters and filters them through the sieve of his own memory and his own erudition.

One part of the meaning of the *Deipnosophists* lies in this link connecting knowledge and the operations, the criteria, the techniques that produce it and make it authoritative and shared in a scholarly community. Quoting, raising questions, answering them, strengthening the link between words and things, checking the coherence of the library, discussing values and meaning—such are the operations underlying the dialogue of Larensius' guests.

I believe such an interpretation sheds some light on Athenaeus' text and could shift the focus for the modern reader. From an indigestible compilation, from an untidy collection of odds and ends, the *Deipnosophists* becomes a lively description of Greek and Roman scholars at work and at play, between the banquet tables and the huge library of ancient Greek books belonging to their host. To summarize my understanding of this text, I would say Athenaeus describes a learned circle of Greeks and Romans bringing back to life the scholarly games and tradition of the Alexandrian Museum, halfway between fun and seriousness, between orality and the world of books, between past and the present of the Roman Empire.

My work on Athenaeus would have been impossible without many conversations and lively exchanges with other contemporary readers of the *Deipnosophists*. David Braund and John Wilkins and all the speakers at the Exeter Conference revealed to me the huge interest and complexity of the text, the difficulty to grasp its meaning, and the many ways one could try to enter and explore this scholarly world. My exchanges with Luciano Canfora, as always, opened many stimulating perspectives, and I am grateful he entrusted the opening essay of the *Deipnosofisti* to me. I would like also to thank Prof. Eugenio Amato and Salerno Editrice who kindly permitted this new English version of my text.

I should also mention my Ph.D. student, Aurélien Berra, who worked on Book 10 of the *Deipnosophists* and on the tradition of *ainigma* and *griphos* in the Greek tradition. As a maître de conférence at the Université de Paris-Ouest La Défense, Aurélien Berra is working on the edition of Book 10 for Les Belles Lettres and on the project of a digital platform for collaborative editing and commentary on the *Deipnosophists*.

This book would not exist without the ongoing friendship, support and generosity of Gregory Nagy, the best of the Classicists I ever met. He deserves all my gratitude for allowing my work to circulate in the American world. I would like to thank too the whole team at the Center for Hellenic Studies in Washington, D.C., for their hard work and support, especially Lenny Muellner.

And last but not least, I am immensely grateful to Arietta Papaconstantinou for her beautiful and elegant translation of the French text and to Scott Johnson for his careful and expert editing work.

Christian Jacob
June 2012

1

On the Art of Planting Cabbage

O N OPENING THE *DEIPNOSOPHISTS* RANDOMLY, the reader could chance upon the following passage (1.34c): "That the Egyptians like wine is also proven by the fact that only there as a custom during meals, before all foods, still today they serve boiled cabbage." Curious, he will continue reading: "And many add cabbage seeds to the foods prepared against drunkenness. And in the vineyards where cabbages grow, the wine becomes less vigorous."

There follow six quotations from comic poets, Alexis, Eubulus, Apollodorus of Carystus, Anaxandrides, Nicochares, and Amphis, all between two and four verses in length. One learns that boiled cabbage is an excellent antidote for the headache of the immoderate drinker; that the Ancients called cabbage *raphanos*, and not *krambē*; that cabbage, eaten in quantity, lightens the weight of one's concerns and dissipates the cloud that weighs down like a shadow on one's forehead (just like wine, one will reflect); and that nevertheless, in truth, against drunkenness there exists no better remedy than a sharp pain, and that cabbage is nothing in comparison.

This particular property of cabbage is further clarified through Theophrastus, the very authoritative peripatetic author of the *Enquiry Into Plants*, who teaches us that the vine cannot tolerate the smell of the cabbage. Thus closes the first book of the *Deipnosophists*, or at least the abbreviated version provided by the *Epitome*, since for this part of the work our only source is the summary of the lost original.

After this first contact with the work of Athenaeus, our reader could have the desire to read a further specimen. He will then by chance open Book 9 and fall on a catalogue of vegetables, and once again on cabbages (9.369e–f): "The cabbage. Eudemus of Athens, in his book *On Vegetables*, says that there are three sorts of cabbage, the so-called "maritime cabbage", the smooth-leaf, and the celery-leaved; in flavor the "maritime" is considered superior. It grows in Eretria, Cumae, and Rhodes, and also in Cnidus and Ephesus. The smooth-leaf variety grows in all countries. The celery-leaved one takes its name from its curliness, for in this respect it resembles celery, as well as in its tendency towards compactness. Theophrastus writes thus: "Of the cabbage (as this is what I mean when I say *raphanos*), there are two sorts, one curly-leaved, the other wild." Diphilus of Siphnos says: "The cabbage which grows in Cyme is very good and sweet, but in Alexandria, on the contrary, it is bitter. Seeds imported from Rhodes to Alexandria produce a cabbage which is sweet for the first year, but after that period they contract the bitterness of the soil."

Further on one learns, through a quotation from Nicander's *Georgica*, that the ancients called the cabbage a "prophet" and asserted that the vegetable had a sacred character. This is borne out, in this case, by the use of the oath formula "by the cabbage" (which functions like "by Zeus") and is documented by four literary quotations. This type of oath, adds Athenaeus, is Ionian. The cabbage, on the other hand, was offered to Athenian parturient women, and served as an enrichment to their diet. After other quotations clarifying the nutritional status of cabbage, Athenaeus passes on to the chard, the carrot, the leek, etc. Our reader will limit himself, for the moment, to the cabbage, and will not be indoctrinated by the encyclopedic catalogue of the universe of vegetables in the cultural, literary and linguistic spheres of ancient Greece. If anything, he will ask himself one first question concerning the status of the text that he happens to have in his hands.

Where does its peculiarity come from? From its inexhaustible inventiveness? From its capacity to develop thematic strands from apparently trivial subjects? From the accumulation of quotations and information that little-by-little delineate the place of the cabbage in the literature, the language, and the social practices of Greece? What sort of space of knowledge, of discourse, of belief, or of cultural values is organized around the cabbage? How does Greek culture look when considered from the point of view of the cabbage?

The cabbage weaves a network of relations and analogies and invites one to pursue a set path from the vine to the celery, from Theophrastus to the comics (comedy writers), from drunkenness to sadness, from cooking recipes to popular medicine, from the religious oath to horticultural techniques, from Egypt to Sybaris, but also from Rhodes to Alexandria, from Ephesus to Eretria. The cabbage thus allows one to glide along texts, to establish connections between quotations, be they direct or indirect, and thus to construct a voice containing Greek knowledge on the cabbage, to a degree that one could answer any possible question regarding the typology, the properties, and the uses of this venerable vegetable.

But who, precisely, is the one curious about the cabbage? Athenaeus? The guests at his banquets? The ancient reader, whose expectations and curiosity are implied between the lines of the text? Or you, perhaps, readers of today, who may be specialists in ancient vegetables or in the history of food and cooking, and who would find in Athenaeus a source of fundamental importance on cabbages? What exactly is the type of knowledge that circulates in the fifteen books by Athenaeus? Is it some Noah's Ark for knowledge that is dead, fossilized in the disorderly accumulation of quotations from books that for the most part are lost? Or is it still active, live knowledge, revealing cultural categories, shared knowledge and beliefs, ways of doing and ways of saying?

By bringing together comical quotations, learned botanists, historians, and authors of specialized monographs, Athenaeus conjures up a universe of flavors and smells, of physical attributes and natural properties: he introduces us to a world of things, of objects, of vegetables, and of gestures belonging to the past but compacted and coagulated into a kaleidoscope of words and quotations. The lost totality, the fragmented image, are recomposed through the juxtaposition of quotations and in the network of correspondences that connect one quotation to another.

The arid mechanics of compilation reveals to the reader the taxonomies of the natural world, that are woven by the threads of symbolic values, of popular or learned knowledge, and of customs: so many cultural mediations that confer meaning to the interaction between humans and the material and natural world. The Greeks are like Bororo Indians of Claude Levi-Strauss: they construct the logical and symbolic coherence of their world through myths, rituals, beliefs, and socially shared observations and knowledge.[1]

Here, it is a library that offers the possibility of reconstructing that cultural universe, and to comment, for example, on the meaningful relations between the vine and the cabbage and on their respective place in the continuum represented by the world of plants. Athenaeus is sufficiently indoctrinated into that culture to intuitively take over its codes and frames of relevance. He still possesses the competence of natives, even if in order to mobilize it he needs to authenticate it through his books. For the reader of today, on the contrary, the distance from such a culture is very great, and its exoticism becomes absorbing.

But what exactly is the register of Athenaeus' discourse? What is his project? And does all this have the blessing of seriousness? Erudite extravagance? Extreme sophistication, that leads to extract and accumulate quotations and information that a reader of Timaeus or Theophrastus would never have noted? Athenaeus introduces an element of disturbing oddity into the heart of a culture and of a library. But is it not perhaps the mechanical stupidity of a primitive search engine that has been programmed to recover everything indiscriminately in the library? Athenaeus would then be a precursor of Bouvard

---

[1]   See Detienne 1994.

and Pécuchet, lost in the labyrinths of language and knowledge, eternally busy mixing words together? Or does he rather exhibit the virtuosity of a pedantic author, who puts together a text from the fragments of the texts of others, who goes beyond the mere mechanics of compilation and extraction, and incorporates the excerpted materials in an enigmatic dialogue, with enigmatic figures, in an enigmatic project?

2

Banquet, Symposium, Library

E VERY READER OF ATHENAEUS, from the very first lines of his work, experiences a perverted Ariadne's thread: by following it, one does not come out of the labyrinth; rather, one progressively penetrates it, one gets lost in its details, losing sight of the overall plan, the architect's project, the structure and purpose of the work. Besides, such is the temptation of every reader of Athenaeus: to stop on the way, on an island of local coherence, whether that is the cabbage, Theophrastus, or the leek, without embarking on that long journey that is the reading of the work in its continuity and integrity. Let us then leave the vegetable gardens of the Greeks to adopt the point of view of Sirius on the labyrinth.

Here we are dealing with learned individuals at a banquet (*deipnon*), assembled at table, that is, on the occasion of festive meals. The *sumposion*, exclusively devoted to drinking, follows the banquet, but the title, *Deipnosophists*, significantly puts the accent on the time of the meal, not on that of the consumption of the wine. At the macro-structural level, Athenaeus' work is presented as the account of a series of conversations held within a scholarly and learned circle meeting in the house of Larensius, a rich Roman patron. Those conversations are distributed so as to adapt to the subdivision of the work in books and to the temporal sequence of the dinner and of the symposium. They accompany and comment on the parade of dishes, followed by the consumption of wine and the pursuits (entertainments?) that are traditionally associated with the symposium.

The symposium is at the same time a social ritual and a literary genre, that have their roots in Greek classical culture, and the fact of referring to one and the other, in Rome, at the time of the Empire's greatest splendor, at the end of the second century of our era, is already significant in itself.

Thus a double argument is in play. On the one hand, Athenaeus' text can be inserted within a literary tradition rendered illustrious, in particular, by Plato's *Symposium*, by that of Xenophon, by Plutarch's *Symposiacs* and his *Banquet of the Seven Sages*, by Lucian's *Symposium*, or *The Lapiths*, or by the episode of the banquet of Trimalchio in Petronius' *Satyricon*.[1] The *Deipnosophists* are inscribed in that tradition, and at the same time assert their originality, and introduce a new form within an already well-attested literary typology. Moreover, they present a critical reflection within and on the tradition to which they belong, either in the form of literary mimesis (for example in the play with the model represented by Plato's *Symposium*), or in the form of explicit discussions. Still, the text of Athenaeus also maintains a relation of homology with the progress of the banquet-symposium itself. That progress constitutes the principle of composition and structuring of the work, in the form of a chronological sequence that leads from the beginning to the end, from the entrées to the *sumposion*, passing through all the courses, all the objects, and all the bits of entertainment that were successively displayed at such meetings. Banquet and symposium are at the same time the argument of Athenaeus' text and its structural principle, the one that regulates the unfolding of the text and the succession of subjects that are brought up in the conversation of the guests.[2]

Indeed, those banquet and symposium conversations do not deal with anything but banquets and symposia. This includes not only those experienced first hand by the guests staged by Athenaeus, but also banquets and symposia in general, insofar as they were social practices constitutive of private or civic life in archaic and classical Greece, or, also, of the munificence of Hellenistic monarchs.

Athenaeus' project would therefore have been to carry to its fulfillment the anthropological and archaeological reconstruction of a social practice that was constitutive of the Greek world, through the reconstruction of a universe of gestures, words, objects, dishes, and flavors, all of which would have been lost if not preserved in the books of Greek authors. His project is an anthropological reconstruction because Athenaeus' intention is to reconstruct the norms, customs, and ethical categories that circumscribed for the Greeks the practice of eating and drinking together, under the eyes of others, within a social and political space, by submitting to the prescriptions of ritualized conviviality.

The *Deipnosophists* is thus a text on a banquet and on a symposium in which banquets and symposia are discussed. A double project becomes manifest. First, to reconstruct, with the help of literary testimonies and historical evidence, a universe of extinct practices and of lost knowledge. Mimesis is at the core of this attempt at cultural *anamnēsis*: the guests of this "dinner" in Rome, staged by a Greek of Egyptian origin, immerse themselves in a cultural universe that

---

[1] On the history of the genre, see Martin 1931:270–80; Dupont 1977; Relihan 1992.
[2] See the very suggestive presentation offered by Lukinovich 1990.

belongs to the past, bears the mark of the Greek tradition and identity, and is codified by works of major importance in Greek literature.

Second, the project consists in the exploration of a universe of language, through examination of the relationship between words and things, since it is a question of recounting in Greek, at the time of the Roman Empire, the course of a banquet and a symposium, of naming the objects and the customs, the dishes, and their flavors. But how, and why, should one delegate these tasks to the guests of a banquet? How can one impose upon a banquet a conversation designed to explore all of its material, social, and cultural aspects? Or, to put it in a single question: how can one drink and eat while discussing drinks and food?

The reflection of Athenaeus' guests on their social practice and on the literary models that make up their background manifests itself at several levels. The *Deipnosophists* is a book on the ritual of the symposium, and provides an assortment of factual information on the dishes, the objects, the practices, and the social norms linked to this form of conviviality. But the mass of information gathered is filtered through the sieve of the library. From the beginning of the work, the delicious banquets offered by Larensius are accompanied by a hyperbolic library of ancient Greek texts, a library that exceeds in extent the most famous book collections of antiquity, even that of Aristotle, of Alexandria, and of the kings of Pergamon (1.3a–b). For Athenaeus, the library represents a field for archaeological excavation, a field for anthropological observation. The anthropologist, here, travels not only through space, but also through time: a single *periēgēsis* transports him to every region of the Hellenized or barbarian world as well as towards the remote past, the time of Homeric heroes, a time whose language and customs must be reconstructed in an erudite game from a distance, from the present. The observer's informers are not natives, but written texts. Yet those books are not lifeless testimonies, and respond in a lively and interactive manner to the questions asked of them. Those questions are formulated and solved thanks to a set of intellectual techniques that allow heuristic crossings from book to book, and within each text, between literary genres, registers of speech and knowledge, between periods, in order to extract from them words and facts and to make them interact with one another. Setting and solving intellectual problems, citing and reciting, challenging each other's erudition, mobilizing the cultural memory and competence of the man of letters, should all be included among the learned entertainments of the symposium. Athenaeus made these activities the dynamic principle of his text.

Thus Athenaeus' characters take a reflective look at their symposium, and at the practice of the symposium in general, but also at their library, where the memory of the Greek symposium lies codified, and at the intellectual techniques that allow one to exploit its deposits of information. They become anthropologists of a culture threatened by oblivion, by the degeneration that affects books, words, objects, customs. Athenaeus' text can indeed be read as a sort of Noah's Ark, wherein a great scholar tries to save all that it is still possible to save, and to entrust its legacy to the long river of history. It is a rescue operation that preserves for us the memory of hundreds of authors and thousands of works which in many cases, without Athenaeus, would have been totally unknown to us.[3]

The *Deipnosophists* lend themselves to several levels of interpretation, depending on whether one is looking for factual information or literary *testimonia*, or whether one is interested in the ways in which this information is called into play, or whether one turns one's attention to the interactive dimension that ensures the unfolding of the work: interaction between the guests, between objects, between books, and between the quotations extracted from them. The highest level of interpretation concentrates on the work itself in its totality, on its structure and on the way it functions, and it is towards that global reflection that I would now like to lead the contemporary reader of Athenaeus.

---

[3] The numbers are those given by Charles Burton Gulick, editor and translator of Athenaeus in the Loeb Classical Library; they should be compared to those of the *Oxford Classical Dictionary*, according to which Athenaeus cites 1250 authors, gives the titles of more than a thousand theatrical works and cites 10,000 verses.

3

"Athenaeus is the Father of this Book"

WHAT WAS ATHENAEUS' PROJECT? Why did he not stop at the stage of compilation, which would have allowed him to possess a collection of excerpts from a wide range of books, or to write a monograph on the pleasures of the table, perhaps even a glossary of the rare words of culinary art? To what end did he build up this mirrored set-up, where the banquet and the symposium diffract into a kaleidoscope of words and information, into a conversation of diners and drinkers exploring the literary memory and cultural knowledge that are specific to banquets and symposia? Why those multiple levels of interpretation? And what do these reveal of Athenaeus' working methods, of his background, of his goals, of the intended recipients of his work, if any?

And first of all: who was Athenaeus? "Athenaeus is the father of this book": these are the opening words of Book 1, in the abbreviated version of the *Epitome*. The title preserved in Marcianus A further specifies that Athenaeus was a native of Naucratis. We know little more about the man than what his work tells us explicitly or allows us to extrapolate.

Athenaeus was a native of Naucratis, a Greek city in Egypt located on the Canopic branch of the Nile, to the East of Alexandria.[1] Founded by Milesian settlers around 620 BC, Naucratis had special status from the reign of Amasi onwards (6th century BC): it was the oldest Greek city founded in Egypt, and it was given its own laws. It is in the region of Naucratis that Plato's *Phaedrus* places the god Theuth, the inventor of calculus, of astronomy, of the game of dice, and of writing.[2]

It was one of the Greek cities of Lagid Egypt, together with Alexandria and Ptolemais. With the foundation of Alexandria, however, it lost its commercial supremacy. Under the Lagids, Naucratis contributed to the cultural growth of Alexandria with a certain number of scholars (the historians Philistus and

---

[1]   On the foundation of Naucratis see Boardman 1980:117–34 and Moeller 2000.
[2]   Plato, *Phaedrus* 274C.

Charon), with authors of *Aegyptiaka* like Lyceas and Dinon,[3] or with the poet Timodemus.[4] In the third century BC, Apollonius of Rhodes had written a *Foundation of Naucratis*,[5] thus rooting the city in the cultural space of Hellenism. Besides, Athenaeus has preserved a fragment of that text, which he attributes to Apollonius of Rhodes "or of Naucratis" (7.283d–e),[6] a sign of the fact that it was important for a Greek city to claim as its own the authors who were born on its soil.

In the imperial period the city was an important center of sophistic culture, whose representatives occasionally emigrated to Athens: that was the case for Proclus of Naucratis, the master of Philostratus. Proclus owned a private library which he shared with his disciples.[7] Among the other sophists who were natives of Naucratis, one should mention, for the second half of the second century AD, Apollonius and Ptolemy, but also Pollux, the author of a *Lexikon*, who was perhaps the model of Lucian's *Master of Rhetoric*; he came to Rome, where among his disciples there was the young Commodus.

Athenaeus is certainly representative of that intellectual environment. A contemporary of Pollux, he shared his interest for lexicography; like Pollux, Athenaeus too came to Rome, and in Rome he remained, contrary to Pollux who, thanks to the protection of Commodus, went to teach rhetoric in Athens. Athenaeus does not seem to have gained familiarity with the imperial family; instead, he entered the circle of a rich Roman of equestrian rank, Larensius, the host of the banquets and symposia staged in the *Deipnosophists*. We are thus in the middle of a patronage relationship that associates a well-known character of Roman society to a primarily Greek intellectual circle, within which, however, there is also no lack of Roman patronyms. In this way, the *Deipnosophists* reflects a social reality in which Rome appears as a pole of attraction for men of letters and sophists of Greek origin. In the second half of the second century AD, Appian of Alexandria offers another example of a scholar of Greek origin attracted by Rome as a place to seek a career. Indeed, those immigrant Greeks put themselves under the protection of cultured Romans who were as rich and as powerful as possible: Appian benefitted from the friendship of Fronto, who obtained for him the position of procurator from the emperor Antoninus Pius.[8] As for Athenaeus,

---

[3] See Fraser 1972:1.511 and 3.736ff., nn. 134–36. Athenaeus cites Lyceas (4.150b; 13.560e and 14.616d).

[4] Fraser 1972:1.582.

[5] Fraser 1972:1.632.

[6] See Aelian, *On the Nature of Animals* 15.23.30

[7] Philostratus, *Lives of the Sophists* 2.21. It is significant that Philostratus does not mention Athenaeus among the famous sophists of Naucratis.

[8] See Swain 1996:248–53; and on Fronto, Champlin 1980.

he dedicated his work to Larensius, a Roman so generous and cultured that he offered lavish feasts to a circle of Greek and Roman men of letters.

We know little more of the personal itinerary of Athenaeus than what is implicit in his text. One cannot but be struck by the significant link that unites his "Athenian" name to his Egyptian origin, but also to a work that is manifestly rooted in the heart of the capital of the Roman empire. That triangle marks the limits of the *Deipnosophists'* cultural space, between Atticism, which re-incarnates a past ideal of language and culture, the Egyptian pole, where through metonymy Naucratis conjures up Alexandria, its library and its immense project of cultural reactivation, and finally Rome, the new center of the world and a center of power where the synthesis, or at least its writing into history can take place. All we learn from Athenaeus is that he had left Egypt a long time ago (7.312a); despite that, Egypt nevertheless represents an emotional and intellectual horizon that underlies the work as a whole.

That emotional horizon manifests itself in the diffuse presence of Egypt in the work, of Hellenistic Egypt rather than the traditional Egypt of the pyramids, the sources of the Nile and the other *mirabilia* (*thaumata*) dear to Herodotus.[9] Athenaeus shows his attachment to his fatherland when he recalls "my Naucratites" (3.73a). In the same way, he remembers that "in my own Naucratis they call *hepsētoi* the small fish that remain imprisoned in the canals when the Nile withdraws from the plain" (7.301c). And when a guest explains in detail the list of wine cups, it is noted that in Naucratis, "the home of our fellow diner Athenaeus," there are several types of cup. This introduces a parenthesis in which one is reminded that many potters were active in Naucratis and that for that reason the gate located in the vicinity of their workshops was called *Keramikē* (11.480d–e). The same local roots probably explain the mention of Naucratis in relation to various subjects addressed in the course of the conversation, be it public banquets on the occasion of religious feasts (4.149d–150a), famous prostitutes (13.596b–d), or the art of flower crowns, concerning which Athenaeus mentions his reading of the work of Polycharmus of Naucratis, *On Aphrodite* (15.675f–676c), the latter being a goddess that was particularly dear to the Naukratites (ibid.). In the course of a long treatise addressed to Timocrates, Athenaeus also evokes "my Alexandrians" (12.541a), which shows the metonymic link between the two cities.

As for the intellectual horizon, there is indeed a strong continuity between the vast cultural project linked to the Library of Alexandria—the gathering of the cultural and literary heritage, along with the classification and quasi-cartographic distribution of the fields of knowledge and of the books

---

[9]   See Thompson 2000.

themselves—and the work of Athenaeus. Alexandria, its library, its erudite techniques and its college of authoritative scholars are very present in the *Deipnosophists*. Both in the library and in Athenaeus' text, one can observe the same intellectual requirements: to inventory, reactivate, classify, enumerate, categorize. Between what was achieved in Alexandria or Pergamon by many generations of scholars and grammarians, and what Athenaeus accomplished in his work, there is thus an undeniable relation of homology, but also of derivation, mimesis, and condensation: the *Deipnosophists* is a condensed library, a Library of Alexandria reduced to the dimensions of a book.

The presence of Athenaeus, however, cannot be reduced to that Egyptian horizon whose summoning suggests a form of emotional and patriotic attachment characteristic of the period. Athenaeus stages himself in his text, at two different levels. In the first instance as one of the diners at the banquets and symposia, where he appears neither as the most talkative, nor as the most sparkling; he maintains his position as a man of letters, and incidentally one learns that he was also the author of a work called *On the Kings of Syria* (5.211a) and a treatise on *The Fishes*, a comedy by Archippus (7.329b–c). Athenaeus belongs in the first person to the library that he browses and explores, and it is not given that his production was limited to those two titles. What's more, one could highlight how those two works, necessarily earlier than the *Deipnosophists*, prefigure the latter's favorite themes, whether that is the lust of oriental monarchs, the consumption of fish, or comic texts.[10]

Secondly, Athenaeus stages himself as the narrator of those banquets for the benefit of Timocrates, a friend who did not take part in them. This type of embedded account is inspired by the architecture of Plato's *Phaedo* and his *Symposium*. It thus inserts the work within the complex dialectics of memory, orality, and writing. Athenaeus recounts to Timocrates, as he remembers them, the progress of the banquet and the content of the conversations of the guests. The guests themselves draw from their memory the recollections of reading: countless quotations taken from books and put into play and into action in the live speech of conversation. There is, therefore, a container-dialogue, that between Athenaeus and Timocrates, and a content-dialogue, that of the deipnosophists, but it is the writing that fixates them both and substitutes the temporality of reading, with the rhythm of the subdivision into books, with that of hearing, which was itself divided into several sections.[11]

---

[10] On those two works see the overviews by Braund 2000 and Wilkins 2000.

[11] See for example 10.459b–c, where Athenaeus postpones to the following day, that is to say the following book, the account of the conversation on drinking wares.

4

Banquet and *Sumposion*

THE SYMPOSIUM (*SUMPOSION*) was an essential moment in the social life of ancient Greece. A circle of friends gathered to enjoy the pleasures of wine, generally after having shared those of the table (*deipnon*), the two being distinct moments.[1]

The time of the symposium is when the guests experience wine, a beverage linked to Dionysus and loaded with his ambivalent and dangerous powers, for the individual as for the social order. The symposium constitutes a socially regulated framework, a framework that makes it possible to share that liminal experience as a group without being subjected to its risks, to touch upon the experience of alterity without losing his own identity. The drinking is part of a social ritual where the pleasures of conversation, song, poetry, games, and *eros* have the task of moderating the effects of drunkenness in a fabric of gestures, attitudes, and rules that place everyone under the gaze of all the others, and under the control of the symposiarch, the master of the symposium. Domesticated in this way, wine reveals every individual's truth and allows a temporary and controlled evasion from the prescriptions and prohibitions of ordinary life. A successful symposium, Lissarague states, is the locus of "good mixing": mixing of the wine, which, in principle, was never consumed pure, but cut with water; mixing of the guests, whose conversation, jokes, and games had to guarantee the harmony of the meeting, the pleasure of all and of each and every one.

That social universe is reflected in the iconography of classical Attic pottery, and especially in the vases that were used to mix the wine (*krātēres*) and on the drinking cups. The wine drinkers saw themselves constantly reminded of the rules of the game they were playing, and the risks to which they exposed themselves if they broke those rules. The literary *testimonia* complete the picture: first of all symposium poetry, where the pleasures of wine and of love find

---

[1] For a good introduction to that fundamental social practice, see Lissarague 1987. On the practice of public banquets in cities, see Schmitt-Pantel 1992.

expression together with the circulation of song and speech within the circle of drinkers, but also the tradition of literary symposia,[2] which use that frame as the setting of an erudite or philosophical conversation. Plato's *Symposium*, Xenophon's *Symposium*, and Plutarch's *Banquet of the Seven Sages* and *Symposiacs* count among the best examples of that literary tradition, which reaches down to Athenaeus himself, and continues with Macrobius' *Saturnalia*.

---

[2]   See Dupont 1994, esp. the first section, "La culture de l'ivresse: chanter pour ne rien dire."

5

An Art of Conviviality
Plutarch and Athenaeus

THERE ARE MANY EXPLANATIONS for the choice of the symposium as the setting of those literary dialogues. The symposium is one of the occasions on which the *philia* of a group of friends will manifest itself. Speech circulates within the group of guests like the cups of wine (1.2a: *epikulikioi logoi*) and creates a space of listening and complicity. The pleasure of the conversation can thus take a serious mode or a playful one, most of the time mixing the two (the *spoudogeloion* is therefore an essential element of literary symposia). Plutarch's *Symposiacs* use the frame of the symposium in a significant way to stage conversations on erudite or philosophical subjects. Is it a literary expedient? Or the reflection of a concrete social practice, where the festive conviviality introduces a complex ritual reactivating cultural memory in the form of a philosophical and learned conversation? At first sight, in Plutarch, the conversation between cultured guests often takes the form of learned dissertations, too studied to be considered the fruit of spontaneous exchanges. We are thus in the space of retrospective writing, of an anamnesis which reconstructs a posteriori the content of conversations held during symposia which are presumed to be real. In any case, Plutarch shows that, at the end of the first century AD, symposia could still be plausibly considered as the scene for conversations taking place between cultured guests. And this leads us to reflect on the definition of culture and on its social and convivial components: *paideia* is shared and tasted within a circle of intellectual and emotional affinity.

For Plutarch, as for Athenaeus, the symposium constitutes the setting for a learned conversation, which mobilizes a number of intellectual practices and disciplines: philosophy, philology, rhetoric, historical erudition, etymology. The experience of wine, as also the specific form of socializing linked to the symposium, are appropriated both for the reactivation of a common cultural memory and for a process of intellectual inquiry which drives the common, and often playful, search for solutions. Culture and knowledge are both subjected to the polyphony of a conversation where the specificity of the interlocutors, their peculiar characters, their professional specializations (rhetors, philosophers of various allegiances, physicians, *periēgētes*, musicians, grammarians, etc.), as well as their intellectual inclinations, make it possible to produce as many points of view, compatible or divergent, on the issues up for debate. Plutarch chose to divide those materials into several distinct symposia; each of those symposia brings together a circle of friends and relatives in a given place for a specific occasion. Every symposium presents the discussion of a particular problem or subject, in this way integrating itself into an overarching work subdivided into nine books, each of which groups together ten questions (only the ninth book, devoted to the Muses, contains a larger group of subjects). The equivalence between a symposium and an issue constitutes the norm, but a given symposium can also lend itself to the discussion of several questions. The work is dedicated to a privileged reader, Sossius Senecio, a high dignitary of the empire, a close advisor of Trajan, twice consul, who had been triumphant over the Dacians. He had with Plutarch a lasting friendship, reinforced by a common philosophical quest. Every book opens with a new homage to that prestigious dedicatee.

In the *Symposiacs*, the setting is more or less elaborate: the symposium frame is set (and sometimes assumed) without being necessarily traced in every detail.[1] The symposium makes it possible to bring together a circle of men of culture, of notables, of relatives, and of friends: the festive conviviality must manifest itself in the form of a disciplined conversation, where the choice of subjects, the dynamics of the exchanges, the form and tone of the questions and the answers are under the control of the symposiarch, who is responsible for the harmony and the decency both of the symposium in general and of its more concrete aspects, like the rules relating to the consumption of wine. As Plutarch observes, the task of preserving the identity and the successful conclusion of the symposium, its conversations, and its entertainments falls to the symposiarch, who must also take care that it not be transformed into a popular assembly or into a sophists' school, if not actually into a gambling joint, a theater scene, or an orchestra (1.4.3, 620b). The symposia of Athenaeus do not always succeed in avoiding such deviations.

Cultural entertainment indeed presupposes a climate of harmony, cordiality (*philophrosunē*), and cooperation in which everyone contributes to the social ritual by virtue both of the word one utters and of the register in which one chooses to utter them. One must be careful not to hurt anyone's feelings,

---

[1] In the *Banquet of the Seven Sages*, the meal is not mentioned, and the banquet as a whole remains surprisingly abstract.

not to disturb the dynamics of the conversation with subjects that are too technical or with polemical affronts, to preserve the specific tone of a conversation that must mix the serious with the facetious without ever offending anyone.[2] Above all, the symposium must bring together *philologoi*, "lovers of discourse" according to F. Fuhrmann's translation, but also men of culture, men of learned and elaborate speech, *pepaideumenoi*, "persons of culture" in Plutarch's words (1.3. 613E). He compares the presence of non-specialists within their circle to the insertion of consonants between the vowels, a necessary condition in order to produce an articulate and comprehensible language.

In Athenaeus, it is a single circle of guests-interlocutors who animate the entire dialogue, which, as we shall see, condenses several banquets. Plutarch, on the contrary, evokes a multiplicity of banquets, distinct from each other through their location, and also through the circumstances that underlie them, or even through the guests whom they bring together. Greek and Roman notables assemble, now guests of one of them, now of another. The nature of the symposia and the circumstances that characterize them delineate the field of a diversified social life within which are combined official occasions, private visits and trips, kinship links, intellectual circles, and spheres of influence. It is notable that Plutarch's learned symposia are situated in Rome and in Greece (Prologue to Book 1), while that of Athenaeus is set in Rome. This location, to which we shall return later, is essential to the understanding of the work.

There are other significant differences between the two authors. First of all, their status, and presence within the work. Athenaeus remains an enigmatic silhouette. Although he is the narrator of the banquets of the deipnosophists, which he attended, he does not play a major role in them, contrary to Plutarch. His intellectual personality comes out implicitly in the work, rather than by asserting itself by virtue of explicit participation in the conversation, or, even less, of adherence to a philosophical school. The *Deipnosophists* delineate a cultural and erudite horizon, a technical competence and a proficiency in learned practices, which contribute to defining the figure of their author and stage director. Plutarch's guests discuss subjects of various kinds. That very variety delineates the shared field of intellectual curiosity, of which the universe of the symposium, with its material, social, ethical, and literary components, constitutes but an aspect. Athenaeus' guests are involved in a game that is at the same time more circumscribed and more complex, a game whose logic we shall try to dissect. They differ from Plutarch's circle where the recommendation to avoid excessive subtleties and polemical confrontation reigned, so as to allow

---

[2]   A fine analysis of this social dimension is given by F. Frazier in his epilogue to the recent edition of the *Symposiacs* (Frazier and Sirinelli 1996:177–207). See also Plutarch, *Banquet of the Seven Sages* 147F–148B.

everyone to participate in the conversation (1.1.5.614D–615A). In the *Symposiacs*, the conversation must remain accessible to all and allow everyone to participate in that activity which is at the same time intellectual, recreational, and convivial. In Athenaeus, on the contrary, for all his erudite and often technical character, despite the difficulty of the issues, there are no cases of exclusion because all those present possess the necessary competence to take part in the game. The interest of the *Deipnosophists* is that it proposes a conversation where, for all the complicity that unites them and for all their command of the same cultural codes and the same intellectual techniques, the guests can nevertheless learn from each other. Plutarch's circle is more heterogeneous, and finds its harmony in the distribution of the guests on the symposium's couches, where, for example, the erudite guest is put next to one who has a desire to learn (1.2.6.618E).

Both Plutarch and Athenaeus invite the modern reader into a two-tiered reflection: firstly, concerning the rules of "living together", on living in society, cordiality, and the care of the other, which manifests itself in the principles of friendship and philanthropy. How is a relation of complicity or involvement constructed and preserved, that principle of congeniality that contributes to the cohesion of a group, its harmony, and its internal regulation? And secondly, they invite one to reflect on the nature and function of culture. Culture does not exist if not in sharing and exchange, in the circumscribing and marking of a shared space, places of knowledge and imagination, a library, the universe of all that was thought, told and written, which is covered following rules of speech assignment, following intellectual techniques for the reactivation of memory.

The mutual exchange within the conversation, the convergence or divergence of points of view, the complementarity of specializations and technical competence, allow Athenaeus' characters to trace constantly new itineraries in cultural memory. The symposium is the place where multiple forms of proximity and distance are experimented with and negotiated: between guests, between them and their points of cultural reference, their memory, their language and their library. Situating a philosophical or a scholarly conversation in a symposium is thus a significant choice, which determines the nature and the scope of the subjects discussed within that setting as well as the mood and the rhythm of the discussion. As Plutarch observes (1.1.2.613B–C), Dionysus, the god who releases and liberates, loosens the reins of language and invests speech with extraordinary freedom. Wine plays its part in determining the tone, the unwinding, the subjects of the learned exchanges between guests: it gives "more passion to the quests and more boldness to the explanations" (7.2.700E). Conversely, thanks to the conversation and to intellectual exercise, and with the help of the Muses, the guests succeed in moderating and containing the effects of drunkenness (8.717A).

6

Larensius' Circle

THE SETTING OF THE CONVERSATIONS is defined from the very first lines of the *Deipnosophists*: the banquets offered by Larensius, a rich Roman, to individuals endowed with the greatest experience in all fields of culture (1.1a). If Plutarch's banquets brought together Greeks and Romans united by bonds of friendship or kinship, and therefore defining a relatively homogeneous social environment of professors and provincial notables, Athenaeus, on the contrary, presents a circle of men of letters enjoying the generous hospitality of a Roman patron. Everything suggests a circle that met regularly, bound by deep complicity, united by common gastronomical inclinations and by similar cultural skills. The cohesion and the dynamics of that group constantly appear in their conversations: the liveliness of the exchanges, the jokes, the challenges, and the disputes, sometimes the invectives, constitute so many indices of a profound familiarity, of a common combativeness concerning culture and the table, where everyone knows how to play the others' weaknesses and strong points to everyone's amusement. Philosophers, physicians, grammarians, musicians, jurists, and sophists are united in a relation of patronage that binds them to a wealthy protector who, in turn, receives them in his house, offering them sumptuous banquets which revive the tradition of the Greek *deipnon* and *sumposion*, and at the same time opening to them his rich library of Greek texts.

The bond that unites Athenaeus and Larensius is of a different order than the one that unites Plutarch and Sossius Senecio. The reality of that relation of social and economic dependence is attenuated, and expresses itself in the conventional language of friendship and hospitality, of munificence and generosity (8.331b–c, 9.381f, 14.613c–d).[1] It is attenuated also because Larensius is himself an authentic man of letters, a perfectly bilingual bibliophile, to the point of mastering the sophisticated codes of his guests, of submitting interesting

---

[1] As rightly noted by Braund 2000b:8; see also Whitmarsh 2000, who puts this situation of social and economic dependence in relation with the treatment on flatterers and parasites in Book 6.

problems to their sagacity, and of contributing to their resolution, with a critical knowledge worthy of Socrates himself (1.2b-c). Larensius loved Homeric poems to the point that he eclipses Cassander, the King of Macedonia, who had even copied them in his own hand and had most of their verses on the tip of his tongue (16.610b). While, during the month of January he was delighting his guests with gourds preserved thanks to a special recipe, he asked them whether the ancients also knew this preparation (9.372d). And since the guests also feed on questions, he suggested one to them: "What do you think the *tetrax* is?" The question finds an immediate answer, a conditioned reflex of the seasoned grammarian: "a kind of bird" (9.398b-c). As we shall see, Larensius was not satisfied with that response.

We see him speak concerning the wild cherry, imported to Italy by Lucullus (2.50f), criticizing his Greek guests for systematically attributing all novelties to themselves; expatiate on the aroma of lentil soup (4.160b); confirm that it was Marius who brought back to Rome the skins of the Gorgons, and that those skins were hanging in the temple of Hercules (5.221f); comment on the number of servants present in Roman families; meditate on the effects of a sumptuary law and on the deterioration of mores in Rome (6.272d-274f). Larensius can quote Clearchus of Soli and his definition of a riddle, describe in detail its various typologies and throw the ball to his companions: when it is impossible to solve a riddle, the penalty consists in drinking a cup of wine. "Now what that cup is, my good Ulpian, try to find out for yourself" (10.448c-e). Opening the conversation on women, a conversation within which prostitutes of fame, their quips and their lovers will hold the place of honor, Larensius praises marriage and begins a detailed critique of the traditions concerning Socrates' bigamy, before evoking the concubines of the kings of Persia and those of the Greek heroes (13.555c-558e). In sum, the host has his role in the learned conversations of the deipnosophists, asserting his knowledge and giving proof of his readings and his familiarity with a library that does not only exist for show. Moreover, he claims his status as a man of letters and scholar, as a member of a learned genealogy that connects him to Varro, surnamed "the Menippean" (4.160c). Larensius is, therefore, a long ways from Trimalchio.[2]

Larensius, who was charged by the emperor Marcus Aurelius to supervise the temples and sacrifices, is presented as an expert in matters of religion (1.2c). He knows the traditional rites, both Roman and Greek, like the back of his hand and is an expert connoisseur of ancient sacrificial ceremonies going back to Romulus and to Numa Pompilius. The ritual of libation, accompanied by a paean in honor of Hygeia, which brings the banquet to an end, is most

---

[2] Braund 2000b:5.

probably accomplished by Larensius, even though the lacunary state of the text does not allow us to be sure (15.702a). He is also a good connoisseur of political laws. He has acquired his competence in the matter by studying the decrees of the assembly and of the Senate, and a collection of laws, all of which are legal texts that seem to be part of his enormous library. In the course of the text, this guardian of traditions mentions his role as procurator of the imperial province of Moesia (9.398e); the temptation is thus great to identify him with the Livius Laurensis who was *procurator patrimonii* at the end of Commodus' reign and contributed to the organization of his funeral on the orders of Pertinax.[3] Thus Larensius was a priest and a high official in the imperial administration. An inscription bears the text of the epitaph dedicated by Cornelia Quinta to her incomparable spouse, P[ublius] Livius Larensius, who exercised the function of *pontifex minor*.[4] Is it our Larensius? Even though the lower-rank priesthood held by the deceased is not incompatible with the hyperbolic praise of Athenaeus, who stresses the competence of his protector in religious matters, one must still explain the absence in the epitaph of Larensius' two procuracies, important administrative posts that should have been mentioned.[5]

Thus Larensius inscribes the *Deipnosophists* in the social reality of imperial Rome. Rich and learned, a priest under Marcus Aurelius, later advancing in the *cursus* of the equestrian order by obtaining under Commodus the charge of *procurator patrimonii* with its high remuneration, he is also the enlightened protector of a learned and scholarly circle which includes Athenaeus. The latter, for his part, devotes to his patron the work that immortalizes his generosity, the splendor of his banquets, the high tenor of the conversations of his guests. A work written in Greek, in honor of that Roman who was bilingual and a lover of Greece, a work devoted to the exploration of the library of ancient Greek books which surrounds the banquet.

By bringing together men of letters from the most diverse regions, by making his banquets a time and a place of accumulation and exhibition, parading courses, dishes, and the most precious objects from all the regions of the empire, by opening his rich library to his guests, Larensius cannot fail to conjure up (to remind one of) the enlightened power and generous munificence of the first Lagids, who at the beginning of the third century BC in Alexandria, founded a Museum and established a library where the intellectual elite of the Hellenized world could be welcomed. Larensius' circle established in Rome a system that was time-tested in the palace of Alexandria: a scholarly community

---

[3]   *Scriptores Historiae Augustae, Commodus* 20.1.
[4]   CIL 6.2126 (=ILS 2932); see Dessau 1890.
[5]   The objection is made by Braund 2000b:7ff,, who suggests we identify the Larensius of the inscription with the father of Athenaeus' host.

which takes its meals in common, devoting itself to letters and knowledge, and sharing a very rich library.[6] If the Lagids collected in Alexandria the heritage of the libraries of Athens and Rhodes, and acquired in particular from Neleus of Scepsis a part of the library of Aristotle, Larensius, by virtue of his acquisitions of Greek books (*ktēsis*: 1.3a), makes of Rome a new Alexandria, and of his house a new Museum, welcoming a cosmopolitan coterie of scholars who are worthy descendants of the inmates of the Ptolemies.

The reference to Alexandria is fundamental in Athenaeus' text, and this at multiple levels. Alexandrian erudition, its scholarly treatises, its *lexika* and commentaries are omnipresent, and among the preoccupations of the Alexandrian scholars and those of Larensius' circle there exists, as we shall see, no break in continuity: the latter like the former were involved in the same activity of inventorying, deciphering, and preserving classical Greek culture; moreover, the Rome of Severus adds a chronological gap of almost five centuries, which makes the undertaking more difficult, but perhaps also more urgent.

The reference to Alexandria can perhaps also be seen in Athenaeus' similes, which we see materialize from time to time; for example, when our author quotes Timon of Phlius and his satire of the Museum of Alexandria, where philosophers were kept like luxury birds in an aviary, a cage of the Muses where the inmates, who live only in their books, argue uninterruptedly (1.22d): is this not a perfect characterization of Larensius' circle, where guests eat while incessantly arguing? Or, when the rare bird first mentioned and then exhibited by Larensius, the famous *tetrax* (9.398b–c), which once again recalls Timon's aviary, resonates with the *tetaroi*, the pheasants that Ptolemy Physcon raised in his palace without ever having dared to eat them (14.654b–c; see also 9.387d). If Ptolemy had seen that a pheasant was served to each one of Larensius' guests, he would have added a twenty-fifth book to his treatise, Athenaeus states. As for Larensius, he has his rare bird cooked to serve it to his guests. When, to our bitterest frustration, Athenaeus does not dwell on the Museum of Alexandria and its library, probably while holding in his hands the rolls of Callixeinus of Rhodes' *On Alexandria*, "since these things are well-known to everyone" (5.203e), does he not suggest the idea that the library and the circle of Larensius, and the text that contains them, are now the new poles of memory and knowledge, the heirs and the substitutes of the foundations laid in Alexandria?

Must I continue to hit the same key? When Athenaeus presents the circle of the deipnosophists, he introduces a Philadelphus of Ptolemais (*Philadelphos te ho Ptolemaeus*), a man brought up in philosophical contemplation, Athenaeus tells us, who in life however has proved himself capable also in the rest (1.1d).

---

[6] See the short description of the Museum in Strabo, *Geography* 17.1.8 C 793–794.

Philadelphus of Ptolemais? He does not appear in the text of Athenaeus that we read today. Instead, it is Ptolemy Philadelphus that appears everywhere in the text: the bibliophile king (1.3b), the king of the procession described by Callixeinus (5.196a, 9.387d, 11.483e–f), the king of the sumptuous ships (5.203c), of immense wealth (5.206c–d), to whom Cleino poured wine (10.425e), who succeeded in deceiving Sosibius, one of his learned *protégés* (11.493e–f), who inspired the fabrication of the *rhuton*, a drinking vase, but also the attribute of the statues of Arsinoe (11.497b); Ptolemy Philadelphus, the king with many lovers (13.576e–f; see also 5.203a; 13.593a–b).

Philadelphus of Ptolemais serves perhaps as a sign. Where does the game begin? And where does it stop? In his presentation of the deipnosophists, Athenaeus tells us: "Plutarch was also present," and he places him among the most refined grammarians (1.1c). Plutarch? One needs to wait until the third book to find out that he comes from Alexandria (3.118f). As for Plutarch of Chaeronea, he appears in the second book (52d), in relation to the only reference Athenaeus makes to the *Symposiacs* (624c): crunching bitter almonds makes it possible to drink much without sinking into drunkenness. When Athenaeus mentions Galen of Pergamon among the physicians present, doubt is no longer an option: Galen "published philosophical and medical works of such importance that he surpassed all his predecessors, and was no less efficient than any ancient author in the art of scientific interpretation (*hermeneia*)" (1.1e–f). Galen was part of Larensius' circle? Athenaeus' emphatic homage suggests that at the very least, he knew the reputation of the physician from Pergamon who, after a first trip to Rome, had taken up residence there permanently from 169 onwards. He remained there probably until his death (around 200?), and thus knew the reigns of Marcus Aurelius, Commodus, and Septimius Severus, three emperors who called upon his services. Galen was one of the great scholarly figures of Rome in the time of Athenaeus and Larensius; he himself belonged to a famous literary circle, that of Iulia Domna, Septimius Severus' second wife, where he could converse, among others, with Philostratus, Serenus Sammonicus, Oppian, and Cassius Dio. Were his treatises, so numerous that Galen himself was obliged to compile an official bibliography of them, a part of Larensius' library? Athenaeus' text does not allow any conclusions regarding this, since his Galen does not practice self-quotation.[7] The guest is also quite less prolix than the author: he speaks on only two occasions, concerning Italian wines, of which he makes a catalogue, describing their properties and effects (1.26c–27d), and concerning breads, sweets, and flours, in a passage where he dwells on their

---

[7] The same is true for all the other deipnosophists: they are guests, readers, interlocutors, but not authors, with the exception of Athenaeus, whose other works are mentioned in the course of the dialogue (5.211a).

taste and their digestibility (3.115c). Medical talk, without any doubt, by a physician who deals with dyspepsia, flatulence, and migraines, which cannot, however, be put in relation with any of Galen's known treatises.[8]

Ulpian of Tyre, one of the dialogue's major protagonists, also awakens a feeling of immediate familiarity: could it possibly be the great jurist, author of a considerable number of works, including a compendium of Roman law reused in the sixth century by Justinian's jurists? Ulpian of Tyre was active under Caracalla (212–217), was exiled by Elagabalus, and was subsequently praetorian prefect under Alexander Severus, before being assassinated in 223 by the praetorian guard. He was also part of the circle of Iulia Domna. However, despite the homonymy, Athenaeus' character does not correspond precisely with that figure: Athenaeus' Ulpian is a rhetor, a virtuoso of the *zētēsis*, that technique of grammatical investigation that animates the entire dialogue. Besides, Ulpian is obsessed with *zētēsis*: he never abstains, neither on the road, nor on a walk, nor in the shops of booksellers, not even in the baths. From this he earned himself the surname *Keitoukeitos*, "is lying there or is not lying there", literally a *mantra* of the obsessive lexicographer, with which he begins practically every time he speaks, preferably when his companions are preparing to try a dish (1.1d–e). The meaning and the use of words haunt him, and there is no respite until he has succeeded in associating every word to a literary quotation that testifies to its usage. Ulpian is the topographer of the Greek language, every word in its place, in one of the library's books.

It is not easy to recognize the traits of the eminent jurist remembered by posterity in this peculiar character. Besides, Athenaeus' silence on what constitutes his glory poses a further problem, since among the deipnosophists are two other legal exegetes, Masurius (14.623e) and Larensius himself.

There is more. The jurist died a violent death, stoned by the praetorian guard.[9] Athenaeus' character also dies, soon after the banquets narrated in the *Deipnosophists*, and the reference to this death, in a future beyond the temporal limits within which the text is contained, gives a particular hue to Book 15, where the simile disappears, abandoning its place to authentic emotion: after a brilliant disquisition on the vegetal crowns that adorn the symposiasts' heads, Ulpian is the first to take leave of the group. He asks the slave for two crowns and a torch, and walks away from the scene. Athenaeus adds: "Not many days after that, as if he himself had predicted that his silence would be eternal, he died happily, allowing no time for illness at all, but provoking great pain to us who were his friends' (15.686c).

---

[8]   See Grant 2000 and Flemming 2000:476, which also shows the abundance of Athenaeus' medical quotations.
[9]   Dio Cassius 80.2.2.

If Athenaeus' character is the praetorian prefect assassinated by his guards, the formulation of the passage is ambiguous. Of course, Ulpian did not die of an illness. But a happy death? Does this euphemism perhaps translate a feeling of fear, a concern for caution on Athenaeus' part, if the drama was still very recent? Does Ulpian's stoning in 223 therefore constitute a *terminus post quem* for the dating of the work? However, Athenaeus' Ulpian dies before Galen, who, despite the chronological uncertainty, was no longer alive when the prefect was assassinated. Moreover, there is no hint at any moment in Athenaeus' character that he had any competence or interest in law. And yet, the similarity of the patronymic and of the ethnic qualification excludes pure and simple coincidence. Athenaeus' character was perhaps the father of the jurist, and nothing prevents us from speculating on the role played by Larensius and his library in the vocation and the education of the younger Ulpian.[10]

The ambiguity of those uncertain identifications opens the way for two divergent interpretations. On the one hand, we can anchor Larensius' circle to a determined time and place, to the reality of a moment of imperial history, under the reign of Septimius Severus, with real people, where it was after all also possible to meet a Philadelphus of Ptolemais. Or else, we can place this circle in a utopia where the living and the dead converse without any concern for plausibility. Such a hypothesis invites one to consider attentively all the patronymics of Larensius' guests. What about, for example, that Democritus of Nicomedia with endless knowledge (1.1d)? And does Aemilianus of Mauritania not evoke Scipio Africanus, also an Aemilianus, famous for his circle of scholars (1.1d)? Do the physicians Daphnus of Ephesus and Rufinus of Nicaea not both refer to one and the same person, Rufus of Ephesus? As for Masurius, he could be the grammarian, contemporary of Tiberius and quoted several times by Aulus Gellius.[11] Zoilus, another grammarian, could remind one of Zoilus Homeromastix, who failed to obtain the gift of a life annuity from one of the Ptolemies (perhaps Philopator), despite the textual criticism he had applied to the *Iliad* and the *Odyssey*.[12] Larensius then offered him at Rome the protection that the Alexandrian sovereign had refused him. In the same way, one could wonder about the identity of that Arrianus *grammaticus*, whose erudition Athenaeus praises (3.113a), or even about that of Varus, another grammarian, whose evokes Varro's (3.118d–e).

The mix of reality and fiction, of history and fantasy, and the care taken to confuse the issues and to play with coincidences, are presumably characteristics of Athenaeus' literary art, fed by multiple influences, from the Platonic

[10] See Braund 2000b:17ff.
[11] I follow here Kaibel 1887:6ff.
[12] Fraser 1972:1.310 and Vitruvius, *On Architecture* 7.*Praef*.8ff.

art of the dialogue to the comic setting. The names of his characters, evoking figures of past grammarians and scholars as they do, while also alluding to contemporaries, were perhaps chosen to awaken echoes and reminiscences in the memories of contemporary readers. However, contrary to what happens in Plutarch's *Banquet of the Seven Sages*, the meetings described by Athenaeus are not inscribed into an utopian framework: they are rooted in a well-determined time and place. We shall not, however, advance any further into this game.[13]

Finally the coherence of the intellectual environment described by Athenaeus should be emphasized. The twenty-two named individuals introduced in the account of Larensius' banquets, who are already present at the beginning of the dialogue, or who appear suddenly as the text unfolds, delineate the field of *paideia* and erudition, with their specializations as physicians, musicians, grammarians, rhetoricians, cynics, or academic philosophers. This is a cosmopolitan environment where one encounters Roman patronymics, like that of the jurist Masurius (a scholar and a poet at the same time), the grammarian Magnus, and the mysterious Aemilianus, next to Greek ones originating from all regions of the Hellenised world: Elis, Alexandria, Nicomedia, Ptolemais, Tyre, Ephesus, Pergamon, Naucratis, Nicaea. Larensius' circle is thus the synthesis of diverse scholarly traditions, those of Alexandria and Pergamon, and that of the Roman world. Every man of letters brings with him to the banquet his culture, his readings, his education, his geographical horizon, and his share of quotations and anecdotes rooted in his home region.

Can Larensius' circle be seen as a new Museum of Alexandria? Like the Ptolemies, Larensius has gathered an elite of scholars who cover all the disciplines of *paideia* (1.1a) and who, beyond their professional specializations, share the same curiosity, the same encyclopedic knowledge. As at the Museum, the scholars take their meals in common—and what meals! Moreover, they have, in Rome, the use of a library which, it would seem, had little to envy from the one at the court of the Lagids and encompassed all the scholarly tradition unfolding from Alexandria to the peak of the Roman Empire.

---

[13] Athenaeus perhaps indicates one of its rules through the leader of the cynical philosophers present at the banquet: "Cynulcus" is his surname ("dog-guide"), and in order to discover the real name of this brilliant cynic (Theodoros) one must wait until Book 15 (692b). Already in Book 4 (160d), Larensius reveals the existence of a birth name that is different from the surname, but without saying what it is.

7

Writing the Symposium

IN THE LITERARY TRADITION of the *sumposion*, writing fixes the ephemeral character of the conversation, and bestows upon live interaction the monumentality of a text that offers itself to reading, to repeated readings, to the intellectual participation at a distance of readers who, even though they did not participate in the symposium, and were not able to take part in the conversation, nevertheless become its witnesses and its audience.

Reading Plato and Xenophon allows us to attend Socrates' symposia and to benefit from them, in so far as it is true that the specific pleasure of the symposium lies in the conversations that are held there, and not only in its material and sensual delights. The philosophical symposium is a place of memorable sayings, and writing perpetuates their effectiveness for generations of readers, while at the same time sketching an ideal scenario for learned conviviality (Plutarch, *Symposiacs* 6.668 B–D).

The reference to Plato in the *Deipnosophists* is at the same time evident and complex. It is evident, as the author of the epitome of Book 1 highlights: "Athenaeus dramatizes his dialogue in imitation of Plato" (1.1f). It is complex, because the imitation of a general model of composition and the literal allusions go hand-in-hand with a number of deviations and variations, more or less important, which markedly differentiate Larensius' banquets from the memorable *sumposion* offered by Agathon. In parallel to the games of mimesis, Plato is also an author who is visibly admired and explicitly quoted; for example, he provides testimony on paradoxal topics (drunkenness, luxury couches, and sane food),[1] but also offers matter for anecdotes, comments, and lively controversies. Through the deipnosophists, Athenaeus in fact abandons himself to a strict criticism of his illustrious model, of his intellectual and moral defects (Book 11), but also of the incoherence and implausibilities of his *Symposium* (Book 5).[2] One

---

[1]   Anderson 2000:320, where the reader is directed to 10.431f, 2.48a, and 4.138a.
[2]   See Trapp 2000.

of the dimensions of Athenaeus' work lies in this critical distance, explicit or implicit, in relation to the founding text of a literary tradition within which he inscribes himself, and in the analysis of the very development of the Platonic symposium, which corrupts the ritual and norms expounded in all their original purity in the Homeric poems (5.186d–193c). Thus the dialogue of the sophists enables a multiplicity of clarifications and points of view on a key author of the classical library, between hagiography and polemics, testifying in this way to the plurality of readings and critical traditions of Plato's *Symposium*.

Without even mentioning the difference of their goals and their contents, the gap between the two works is obvious. There is a difference in physical dimensions, the fifteen books of the *Deipnosophists* being no match for Plato's *Symposium*. The dialogue between Athenaeus and Timocrates frames every book or almost, offering thematic points of reference to the reader, and allowing him, by virtue of the announcement of the subject that will be treated in the following book, to read the rolls in their proper order. There is a difference in the genesis and the transmission of the account of the symposium, since in Plato, Apollodorus' friend obtains a first report by an anonymous informer, himself holding the information from Phoenix, son of Philip, while Apollodorus has heard the account directly from the mouth of Aristodemus, the prime source for this oral tradition (172a–b). With Athenaeus, Timocrates has a direct witness of the meeting of the deipnosophists, a witness who, moreover, does not seem to be giving his first report (1.2a). Athenaeus thus occupies the position of Aristodemus, not that of Apollodorus;[3] and the name of Timocrates recalls that of Echecrates in the *Phaedo*.

The most impressive difference between the two texts, however, resides in the treatment they give to the *deipnon* and the *sumposion*, that is to the meal and to the time dedicated to the consumption of wine. In Plato, the banquet proper is mentioned without being described in detail (175c and 176a): the dialogue proper opens when the guests are preparing to drink. The dinner is not a place for memorable words. The banquet that inaugurates Xenophon's *Symposium* also takes place in silence, even if that silence has its explanation in the beauty of the young Autolycus, who conquers all the guests (1.9–11). Of the banquet proper, however, we know nothing at all. Plutarch remains loyal to that model: his *Symposiacs* are speeches made with a cup in one's hand, not with one's mouth full. Only once the meal is finished do they begin to talk (5.672E). Athenaeus, on the contrary, devotes the first ten books of his work to the banquet. The *sumposion* begins with Book 10 and occupies the last third of the work. This shift of

---

[3]   From that point of view, the prologue of the *Deipnosophists* presents more similarities with that of the *Phaedo* (57a). One can compare this with the beginning of Plutarch's *Banquet of the Seven Sages* (146B), which presents another variation on the Platonic model.

focus is further underlined by the title chosen by the author: "deipnosophists", "the scholars at table". Here the episode of the banquet predominates, and the succession of dishes served constitutes, as we shall see, one of the structuring principles of Athenaeus' text. If the reported conversation starts well before the time of the *sumposion*, speaking while eating, and above all, speaking of food during the meal, turns out to be problematic.[4]

Finding inspiration in Plato's "dramaturgy", Athenaeus recounts the meeting of Larensius' circle to an interlocutor who has not participated in it. Timocrates is the substitute of the reader, the one who by virtue of his curiosity and of the friendly pressure exerted upon him, encourages the narrator to delve into his memory and to bring forth the account. Like in Plato's *Symposium*, the reported account has the power to turn the audience and the reader into participants, to integrate them into that circle of learned complicity, of speech and of memory. One could ask whether one of the aims of Athenaeus' work is not to turn Timocrates, perhaps a substitute of the reader, into a deipnosophist, by making him enter, in turn, that game of culture and conviviality, by providing him with the codes and materials that are necessary in order to participate in those sophisticated conversations. As for Plutarch, he offers to Sossius Senecio the written account of the conversations of the symposia in which (or at least in some of which) he had participated. However, the insistent presence of the dedicatee, especially in the prologues of each book, cannot hide the fact that Plutarch also had in mind a wider readership (see 2.629C–E).

The literary form of the symposium conversation gives a new scope and a new significance to the social game that is represented in that way. The game becomes the setting of a literary, philosophical, or scholarly project, and the literary form can constitute its essential element, or just a superficial background that will be already forgotten as it is displayed. The conversation born within the context of shared and controlled drinking deserves, according to Plutarch, to escape oblivion, to be fixed in memory. To make this point, he rests on illustrious precedents: Plato, Xenophon, Aristotle, Speusippus, Epicurus, Prytanis, Hieronymus, and Dio.

In Plutarch, the symposium conversation combines with the tradition of the Platonic dialogue, although it takes the form of a series of learned dissertations, putting together a dossier of sources and arguments on a given subject. The subjects treated in the *Symposiacs* include two large groups of questions: those that refer directly to the symposium, and others, of literary, historical, philosophical, medical or scientific nature, which reflect a curiosity with a wider scope. Here are examples of the second category of questions, which

---

[4]   See Romeri 2000:263ff.

Plutarch defines as "symposium talk" (2.629C–E, preface: *sumposiaka*): "Why do old people read letters better from a distance?" (1.8); "Why are clothes washed better with fresh water than with sea water?" (1.9); "Who was born first, the egg or the hen?" (2.3); or, "Who is the god of the Jews?" (4.6). As for the first category, it has, according to Plutarch, a practical function: to formulate and to make explicit the rules of the symposium, the principles of making it run smoothly, its values. The conversation allows the guests to give new blood to the tradition, to reach a point of agreement on the progress of their meeting, to collectively define its rules, inscribing it, at the same time, in an archaeology of cultural and social practices that hinges, in particular, on the precedent constituted by literary and philosophical symposia. Examples among others of those "symposium questions" (2.629C–E; Preface, *Sympotika*) are: "What are, according to Xenophon, the questions and the jokes that are pleasing or displeasing during a symposium?" (2.1.1.629E–F); "On the art of asking questions" (2.1.2.630A–B); "whether flower crowns are necessary at the symposium" (3.1); "why does sweet wine not cause drunkenness" (3.7); "should one or should one not filter wine" (6.7). It is noteworthy that the discussion can also focus on the significance of ancient Roman usage (7.4: "why did the ancient Romans have the habit of not having empty tables or burnt out lanterns taken away").

The deipnosophists participate in the same reflection project: it is a question of integrating the gestures, the objects, the codes, and the distractions of the symposium within a network of quotations, words, anecdotes, authorities, and explanations; of placing drinking and drunkenness under the control of the social ritual of conversation, of making them subject to discourse and to memory. To the calm and well composed talks of Plutarch's friends, however, Athenaeus substitutes a continuous and dazzling flux of exchanges, words, and quotations, of erudite disquisitions and of anecdotes, which spread through each of the fifteen books. The very structure of the dialogue at times drowns in an impressive logorrhea (or, as Cynulcus put it, "logodiarrhea": 4.159e), with the consequence that the reader is led to suspect that the text is structured according to different principles.

8

Forms of Collection

THERE ARE WORDS that allow one to obtain a view from above the labyrinth, to seize one of its principles of structural coherence. For example *sunagōgē*, which means "collection". It is one of those keywords that invite one to unravel Ariadne's thread in Athenaeus' labyrinth. Indeed, not only does the activity of collection appear, it is one of its constitutive elements.

When Athenaeus turns to Timocrates at the end of Book 2 to put an end to his catalogue of vegetables and of quotations relating to them, he uses the word *sunagōgē* (2.71e); likewise, at the end of Book 11 (509e), when the catalogue of wine cups has just been given. *Sunagōgē* also describes the assembly of scholars at the Museum of Alexandria (5.203e), as it does that of the guests at the symposium (5.192b).[1] Moreover, the neuter plural *sunagōgima* is sometimes used as a synonym for "banquets", and *sunagōgion* for "symposium" (8.365b–c). As a quotation by Antiphanes shows, three guests are "gathered" on a *triclinium* (2.47f). It is, however, also texts that are "gathered", for example playful epigrams (2.321f). *Sunagōgē* can be used of a lexicon, that is of a collection of words (7.329d; see also 1.5b). This passion for collections of words is also characteristic of Ulpian: he "collects thorns" (i.e. thorny questions) in everything he runs into (3.97d). *Sunagōgē* is used, more generally, for any erudite collection (9.390b; 13.579d–e, 609a). Books can also be collected (in which case one has a library). Larensius, with his *sunagōgē* of books, surpasses all his most illustrious predecessors (1.3b; see also 12.515e).

Collecting, gathering, and accumulating are essential gestures in Athenaeus' universe. Larensius' guests are a gathering of scholars that recalls the Museum of Alexandria. Larensius' library, that prodigious collection of books, constitutes the horizon of the banquet. It is also the horizon of Athenaeus' text, a text that is at the same time a compendium and a map of the library. The *Deipnosophists*

---

[1] On "assembling" a dinner party or a banquet, see also 4.143a; 5.186b, 187a, 187f, 211c 216f; 6.246c; 10.420e.

contains collections of facts, of quotations, of texts, but also of words and of things. Athenaeus' text is at the same time a symposium, a library, a collection of curiosities, and a lexicon.

9

Accumulation and Structure

A THENAEUS' WORK, with everything it includes (objects, quotations, infor-mation, words), is indeed a collection that seems destined to perpetual growth. That collection, however, and the text within which it finds its space, are nevertheless organized on the basis of ordering principles.

The work's prologue, in so far as it is only preserved by the epitome, announces its content (1.1a–c):

> [Athenaeus] introduced fish into the work, with the related ways of preparing them and the explanations of their names; multiple vari-eties of vegetables and animals of all sorts; authors of history, poets, and scholars in every field, musical instruments and innumer-able types of jokes, and he has included in his exposition the differ-ences between cups, the riches of kings, the sizes of ships, and other subjects, so numerous that it would not be easy for me even to recall them to memory: the entire day would pass expounding one genre after the other. Also, the general design of the work tries to imitate the sumptuous abundance of the banquet, and the articulation of the book mirrors the menu served in the course of the discussion. Thus is presented the delightful banquet of words staged by Athenaeus, who is the admirable inventor of the general design of the work and who, surpassing himself like the Athenian orators, he raises himself with the ardor of his eloquence step by step through the successive parts of the book.

These few lines offer a real key to the understanding of the work. In the first place they define its contents. Athenaeus' book includes things, names, classifications, but also other books. One of its unifying threads will be to connect all those different elements to each other, to circulate, that is, between the things, the words, and the texts that convey them. The heterogeneous *bric-à-brac* in which one finds vegetables, fish, boats, drinking cups, and jokes is in fact governed by a specific order, that of classificatory reason, which imposes on accumulation the distribution into categories, genres, and subgenres, a form of intellectual mechanics that can be applied as much to the typology of kitchenware as to that of jokes or vegetables. It is thus possible to conciliate ordering principle and infinite variety, in what the text calls "the general design of the *logos*." Athenaeus' role is precisely that of a "manager of the discussion," in charge of ensuring the succession of subjects, without repetitions and without omissions, just as the administrator of the banquet deals with the proper succession of the dishes. The deeper issue in the work lies in conciliating its antithetical requirements, the pleasure of the collection, the *sunagōgē*, and the assertion of order—*taxis*—which allows one to circulate within the collection and to follow a trajectory that is as coherent as the one within classifications and texts, or the one that leads from the *apéritif* to the final libation of a symposium.

This preamble thus establishes the principle of a structural mimesis that involves the conversation, the book, and the banquet; the latter element brings to the first two a general ordering principle. That principle deploys a space of homologies and correspondences between distinct levels: the unfolding of the banquet and the text's thematic sequences; the dishes and the words that serve to describe them; the words of the banquet and the banquet of words; the conversation of the guests and the written dialogue, reconstructed from memory (presumably) by Athenaeus; the quotations from comedy and the comedy played by the guests on the stage of the banquet; the banquet of the deipnosophists and the banquets mentioned in their conversations, from Homer to the Hellenistic kings; the *Deipnosophists* as a text inscribed in the tradition of symposium literature.

This "economy" of the text manifests itself on a series of levels. The present distribution of the *Deipnosophists* in fifteen books corresponds without doubt to the author's project, since the beginning and the end of each book are almost always framed by the dialogue between Athenaeus and Timocrates, the former recounting to the latter the banquets of the sophists and the development of their conversation.[1] The continuity of the banquets is thus broken up into sequences that correspond to the succession of the phases of Athenaeus' narration to his friend, and to the subdivision of the work into distinct volumes. Those initial, and sometimes final, markers, distributed throughout the fifteen books undercut the thesis advanced by some that Athenaeus' work initially comprised thirty books and was later abbreviated to the form in which it has come down

---

[1]   It is also significant to note how these structural elements have disappeared in the *Epitome*, where the name of Timocrates is only encountered once: 1.2a.

to us. This hypothesis is based on eleven notes in uncial script contained in the Marcianus A, which refer to a division of the work into thirty parts. The most likely explanation is that one of the copies forming the basis of that manuscript had been copied on thirty rolls, and that each of the fifteen books occupied two rolls.[2]

To this first organizing principle, which involved the distribution of the material into the fifteen sections that made up the work, a second structural criterion can be added: the unfolding of the banquet and the symposium. The most important points of articulation are easy to locate: up to the end of Book 5 we see the parade of hors d'oeuvres. From Book 5 to Book 10 the main courses of the banquet are served. From Book 10 onwards (422e) begins the *sumposion* proper, devoted to drinking and to its entertainments. These points of transition are often highlighted by the narrator, and sometimes also by one of the guests.

A third organizing criterion, intertwined with the major principles of subdivision I have already mentioned, is that of thematic distribution, that is, the parade of foods, dishes, objects, and entertainment, but also the more general subjects of conversation related to the history of banquets, to their norms and to all the related cultural problems. To this principle of thematic variety there adheres a formal variety in the exposition. Indeed, the all-encompassing form of the dialogue integrates levels and genres of discourse that are quite different from each other: for example, very extensive quotations, which could be the pure and simple transcription of extracts of other works, sometimes even an entire text; or lexical sequences which, starting from a lemma, align quotations and comments; or autonomous disquisitions of variable length, which interrupt the dialogue, even in the cases when they are attributed to one of the guests.

The following table offers a summary of the main subjects treated by Athenaeus, at the macro-structural level, obviously without giving an account of all the digressions and meanderings of the dialogue:

Book 1 The circle of Larensius; elements of symposium bibliography; the lifestyle of Homer's heroes; wines and specialties of the Greek cities.

Book 2 Wine and water; the dining room and its furniture; fruit; appetizers and what is nibbled to accompany them.

Book 3 Seafood; tripes; fried food; bread; salted fish hors d'oeuvres; *libum* and chickpea bread.

---

[2] See the discussion by Arnott 2000 and Rodrigues-Noriega Guillén 2000.

Book 4   Famous banquets and symposia; strangeness and extravagance; lentil soup; critique of the philosophers; the cook and his tools; the hydraulic organ and other musical instruments.

Book 5   Public banquets and symposia of the Greek cities; the Homeric symposia; critique of Plato's, Xenophon's, and Epicurus' literary symposia. Banquets, processions, and vessels of the Hellenistic kings.

Book 6   Fish; luxury; the parasite and the flatterer; slaves.

Book 7   *Opsophagia*; alphabetical catalogue of fish; Epicurism, a philosophy of pleasure and the stomach; famous cooks and boasters.

Book 8   Fish: *mirabilia*, jokes, famous fish-eaters; the point of view of naturalists and physicians.

Book 9   Cold cuts; vegetables; meats: domestic fowl, suckling pig, etc; Larensius' *tetrax*; game. The cook and his art.

Book 10   On frugality; wine mixtures, drunkenness, thirst, great drinkers; enigmas and riddles.

Book 11   Alphabetical catalogue of wine cups; on the literary genre of the dialogue; critique of Plato: errors, malevolence, doctrine, political influence.

Book 12   *Truphē* and pleasure; peoples, Greek and barbarian kings, political figures devoted to *truphē*; philosophers and *truphē*.

Book 13   On women; famous prostitutes of the past, their witty lines, their lovers; eros and beauty.

Book 14   "Second tables" and desserts: sweets, fruit, poultry, cheese; the art of the cooks.

Book 15   The cottabus, crowns, perfumes; Attic *scolia* and the paean, parodies; lamps.

At a fourth level, Athenaeus' text is structured by the dialogue of the guests. If the framing dialogue between Athenaeus and Timocrates underlines the distribution of the work in fifteen "volumes", the dialogue between the deipnosophists, recounted from memory by Athenaeus, leaves room for a multiplicity of levels and forms of enunciation and multiple modes of statement, depending on the identity, the character, the intellectual interests, and sometimes the profession of the interlocutor: indeed, grammarians, physicians, musicians, and philosophers all explore the complementary facets of the same cultural universe, and bring it back with a shared effort of recollection and mobilization of knowledge. This interaction contributes to the dramatization of the banquet, and to the game of mimesis with the universe of comedy, amply represented in the quotations of the guests. The dialogue, in fact, is not limited to distributing the quotations among a plurality of voices and to break the monotony of the compilation. The conversation is the motor of a process of reactivation of cultural memory. In this codified social game, the circle of participants cooperates towards a common task, circulating the words, the questions and the answers, in the same way in which the dishes and the wine circulate among them. The dialogue has a structural role, not only in the organization of the work as a whole, but also in the production of knowledge, and in the formulation of contradictory, and sometimes problematic, opinions and points of view on values, norms, codes of linguistic, cultural, ethical, and social relevance.

In this respect, two protagonists play an essential role: Ulpian and Cynulcus. Their often lively exchanges and their invectives, whose excessive sharpness in itself brings out their playful and codified nature, brighten up the uninterrupted flux of literary quotations and erudite notes with scenes of pure comedy.[3] One could also claim that implicitly they regulate and problematize it, offering a thoughtful and sometimes critical point of view on the unfolding of the conversation and on the very project of Athenaeus. The obsessively inquisitive Ulpian and Cynulcus, the leader of the cynical philosophers, become angry, hit their cushions, threaten to walk away, hurl invectives and challenges at each other, poke fun at each other, bringing into question Athenaeus' enterprise, the meaning of his work, and the legitimacy and relevance of his search for words and meaning. What is the point, in the end, of this perpetual sifting of Greek literature in search of rare words and of their usage, in search of a proper Attic language that no longer corresponds to the state of spoken Greek? Cynulcus exclaims: "You do not know how to sustain continuous and wide-ranging discussions, nor recall the facts of history … but you waste all your time investigating this nonsense: 'Is it written or is it not written? Has it been said or has it not been said?'. And then you examine pedantically all the arguments that are presented in the speeches of those who are in dialogue with you, collecting the thorns [the thorny passages] … without ever putting together any of the more beautiful flowers" (3.97c). Lexicography has nothing to do with anthology. Ulpian replies by treating the cynic as an enraged dog, citing new authorities, and intimating that Cynulcus should answer a question if he wants to avoid a

---

3   See Wilkins 2000c.

sound beating (3.100b). Upon the arrival at the table of fried livers wrapped in intestine membranes (*epiplous*), Cynulcus nags Ulpian: "Tell me, learned Ulpian, if in some place wrapped liver can be named in this way." "If you tell me first in which author *epiplous* is used to describe the grease and the membrane" (3.106e). A little further, while Ulpian is deriding Myrtilus, Cynulcus interrupts him, screaming: "We need bread!" (3.108f); at that point the conversation shifts from fried fish to the art of bread-making in Greece. When Cynulcus requests to drink *decocta* (in Latin in the text), it is Ulpian who becomes angry and hits his cushion: "When will you stop expressing yourselves through barbarisms? Perhaps only when I will have abandoned the symposium and will have gone, since I am unable to digest what you are saying?" To which Cynulcus replies, "Living presently in Rome, the queen of the empire, my dear, I used the local language out of habit" (3.121e). These words do not lack good sense when confronted with the Atticist purism of the lexicographer. And when the *libum*, a sweet flat bread, is served, Cynulcus provokes the Syrian Ulpian once again: "Fill yourself with your *khthōrodlapson*, a word that, by Demeter, is not found in any ancient author, except in your compatriots, the Phoenician writers." "But for me, horsefly that you are, I have had enough of sweet flat bread and honey," is Ulpian's answer (3.125f–126a).

In Book 6, immediately after an important speech by Democritus on slavery, Cynulcus suggests it is finally time to eat: "I am very hungry, seeing that until now I have eaten nothing but words" (6.270a). Ulpian, continuously waging war on him, replies: "Beautiful speeches are food for the soul" (270c). Cynulcus answers and pretends he is leaving, but at that point fish is served and Cynulcus, having dealt a blow to his cushion and let out his rage with a bark, decides to stay (270e). It is true that the end of Book 6 is now close. At the beginning of Book 7 Cynulcus is in a better mood, and asks Ulpian: where is there a mention of the feast of the *Phagēsia* and the *Phagēsiposia*? Ulpian does not know, enjoins the slaves to suspend the service, and asks the Cynic to give the answer, which the latter does with erudition (7.275c–276a).

In Book 8 there is another incident, when Democritus suggests a new research subject for Ulpian. Cynulcus bursts out: "And which one of these, I shall not say fish, but problems, is he not capable of understanding? All he does is select and extract the bones of the odds and ends and the small fish, and of the tiny and even more miserable fish, if there are any, disregarding the large slices of salted fish." For Cynulcus, "Ulpian does not feed himself with human food, but observes those who are eating, in case they happen to discard a fish-bone, a bit of bone or cartilage" (347d–e). In short, the dog is not the cynic, but that lexicographer who is always picking holes in something.

Cynulcus is a guest who shouts a lot and uses invective according to the rules of the art of the Cynics, for example when he calls Myrtilus a pornographer (this is where the word enters western literature), accusing him of hanging around taverns in the company of prostitutes, bringing along the books devoted to them (13.566f–567a). To reply, Myrtilus throws himself into a beautiful eulogy and a long list of women with dubious virtue but with lively spirit and famous lovers, while at the same time re-establishing his reputation: *erōtikos*, yes; *erōtomanēs*, no (599e). After that flowing speech, much appreciated by everyone, Cynulcus adds, ironically: "There is nothing more empty than erudition!" (610b). This is a paradoxical statement, since Cynulcus quotes the words of the divine Heraclitus. Cynulcus continues: "What is the use of all those names, our dear scholar, if not to obtain the effect of overwhelming the hearers, rather than to make them wise?" (610c). It is indeed time to ask oneself this question, after thirteen books of grammatical wanderings of all sorts. That earned him a series of blows, together with a violent diatribe against philosophers in general, and the Cynics in particular.

The duet Ulpian-Cynulcus is in keeping with the dialogue's comic resources. The Cynic often takes the initiative, animated by a constant aggressiveness vis-a-vis his Syrian companion (15.669b, 701b). Yet there is no hate between them: they are only playing a game in which each one holds on to his role and looks at the other sideways in order to encourage him to develop his act (15.671b; see also 697b–e). Their exchanges, putting an end to a sequence or inaugurating a new one, often allow a change in theme in the course of the conversation. They regulate the dialogue, renegotiate its form and purpose, embody its deeper tension: to quote or to eat?[4] Their effect is also to subject to inquiry their language, their own practice as deipnosophists, the validity and relevance of their speeches, and their knowledge, with an obvious component of self-derision. All things considered, however, Cynulcus sits quite well in his place at the sophists' banquet: he too likes to rummage through books hunting down their secrets (15.678f). He too has the memory of an elephant, capable of correcting the grammarian Myrtilus who has read the twenty-eight books of Phylarchus' *History* without noting the passage where the author states that in the cities of Cos there are neither prostitutes nor *aulos* players. "Where does Phylarchus say that?"— "In the twenty-third book," answers Cynulcus without hesitation (13.610d). Cynulcus really deserves the title of *grammatikōtatos* (5.184b).

It would be tempting not to reduce the dialogue to the interaction of the guests, but to extend it to all the Greek authors cited in the course of their

---

4   Wilkins 2000c:26.

conversations; the remnants of their texts, the reported words, deploy a complex polyphony, almost a dialogue of the dead, where Homer, Theophrastus, Aristotle, Polybius, Poseidonius, Alexis, and a hundred others converse through the medium of quotations. This can be seen as the fifth level of organization of the text: the possible encounters between the authors of the books ordered on the shelves of the library (that of Larensius?), that utopian space of memory, where words and thoughts set in writing are stored, are here set in motion, awakened, activated by the memory and the voices of obsessive readers who contribute to the construction of a text-*corpus* of undeniable originality.

Indeed, only a hasty reader could perceive in the *Deipnosophists* nothing but a haphazard and disorderly flux of textual materials chosen along the way of a lazy and thoughtless compilation. To the attentive reader, on the contrary, the work follows the principles of a complex architecture, both at the level of its great structural divisions and at that of its micro-sequences. It cannot be doubted that an authorial project gave form to the materials gathered from books, and the work thus constructed produces meanings that cannot be reduced to those produced by the quotations that are embedded in it.

For that reader I would like to lead the way in the following pages, by showing that the work of Athenaeus defines an original system of textuality, both from the point of view of writing as from that of reading. The links, the path, and the crossroads all play a fundamental role in it: they make it possible to circulate without end, and without getting lost, in the labyrinth of words, through the web of Athenaeus.

10

Serving the Dishes, Quoting the Texts
The Unfolding of the Banquet

O NE OF THE THREADS of Ariadne that allow a reader to circulate within that labyrinth is constituted by the very development of the banquet and the parade of dishes. Athenaeus took care to underline the most important points of reference, in the form of a comprehensive account that delineates the general framework of the guests' conversations.

The guests take their places and lie down on the symposium couches as they please, without waiting to be given a place by the superintendent of the banquets, the *onomaklētōr* (2.47e). In his *Symposiacs*, Plutarch nevertheless called attention to the necessity of seeing to the careful placing of the guests, with the aim of ensuring the success of the conversation (1.2: "On whether the host must himself see to the seating of the guests, or on the contrary leave them the freedom to choose"; see also 5.5.678C). Athenaeus' guests, however, form a much more homogeneous group than Plutarch's; the latter's success presupposed that contiguities were finely studied, with the aim of preserving the collective dynamics of the conversation, ensuring, for example, that next to a scholar would be seated a person who wished to receive instruction (1.2.6.618E).

The gathering of Larensius' circle is put under the authority of a symposiarch (4.159e), the same Ulpian, who is also described as "superintendent (*tamias*) of banquets" (2.58b).[1] We have few indications on the place of the banquet as such, or on the furniture. The incessant parade of slaves and cooks, however, reminds us that we are in the house of a rich individual, whose munificence Athenaeus highlights several times.

One can presume that once they were lying on the couches, the guests were presented with a tablet (*grammateidion ti*) containing the dinner's menu, with the dishes that the cook was getting ready to prepare. This usage is mentioned

---

[1]   On the role of the symposiarch see Plutarch, *Symposiacs* 1.4.

in general terms in the compendium of Book 1 (49d). That "tablet", for us readers, is nothing other than Athenaeus' work itself. And the menu, precisely, is the connecting thread of both the text and the meeting, the "programme" of the banquet and of the conversation.

First of all, Larensius' guests take an *apéritif* (2.58b: *propoma*). As for the dinner, it opens with hors d'œuvres like salted fish (3.116a), but the dinner proper only begins in Book 4, as announced by Athenaeus (3.127d). Ulpian indicates its end: "Once we have finished eating (*epei dedeipnamen*)," dwelling on the specific verb form he used for the occasion, with great deployment of comic quotations (10.422e). At that point the symposium can begin: "The time has come for us to drink!" (10.423b–c); Ulpian gives the example, emptying his cup and proposing a toast (10.425f–426b). After his long typological list of wine-cups, which remains, in this respect, a passage of reference for modern archaeologists, and accompanied by applause, Plutarch makes a libation to the Muses and to their mother, Mnemosyne, Memory, and drinks to everyone's health (11.503f). Larensius had taken care to enliven the symposium with various types of entertainment, like, for example, those jesters who then become a good subject of conversation to the guests (14.613c–d). What's more, that fine connoisseur of Homer had not missed this occasion to bring rhapsodes who would recite his favorite poems (14.620b). Since wine revived the appetite, it was common also to serve a whole series of sweets and delicacies, which the ancients called "second table", and which to the reader, who has been satiated for a while, look similar to a second meal (14.639b). The servants then bring crowns and perfumes (15.669c, 676e), which confer a certain lightness to the conversation of the last book, augmented by the fact that crowns and perfumes are accompanied by songs, the Attic *skolia* (693f). When Ulpian and Cynulcus have already gone, the symposium comes to a close with libations and with the singing of a paean.

The incidents that occur during the meal are rather rare, and have the function of introducing shifts in direction, or even real breaks, in the subjects of conversation. When the guests hear the sound of a hydraulic organ played in the vicinity, the conversation passes very naturally from sacrificial cuisine to that instrument, thanks to the intervention of the musician Alcides, incited by Ulpian to speak on the subject (4.174a–b). The sound of flutes, the noise of the cymbalum and the rumble of the drums, accompanied by songs, resonating throughout the city, mark the celebration of the feast of the Parilia, which commemorated the foundation of Rome every year on 21 April (8.361e–f).

The late arrival of the citharode Amoebeus during the symposium—the meal having finished for some time—is the occasion of a scene of comedy in the form of a sophisticated exchange of quotations with the cook Sophon: the citharode is invited to join the company, and having drunk a glass of wine he begins to sing while accompanying himself on the cither and earning every-one's admiration (14.622d–623d). Shortly after, Masurius' long digression on music ends on the low-pitched sound of an *aulos*, and the music-loving jurist concludes by quoting verses from Philetairus' *Man who Loved the Pipes*: "Oh, Zeus, how nice it is to die to the sound of the pipes..." (14.633e). Towards the end, the *sumposion* is invaded by tumult (15.669b), but it does not turn into a *kōmos* of pleasure-seeking merrymakers as in Plato's *Symposium*, where Alcibiades made his memorable entrance in quite the same way (212c–213a). Ulpian is the first to leave the party, having asked for two crowns and a torch (15.686b). A theatrical exit that bears the mark of nostalgia: his imminent death places the banquet at a time that is now past. Without Ulpian, Cynulcus would be less brilliant and Larensius' circle would lose its symposiarch and entertainer. Thus all the other deipnosophists leave, asking the slave for a lantern as night has fallen in the meantime (15.699d); soon after, Cynulcus also leaves, after a last allusion to the beautiful Agathon of Plato's *Symposium* (15.701b).

The ballet of servants bringing dishes gives rhythm to the progression of the banquet as to that of the conversation (6.224b, 262b). Sometimes it is the cook in person who enters the scene—a traditional resource of comedy—to show he is learned in sophistics, rhetoric, and his art: thus he appears to comment on his half-roasted, half-boiled pork (9.376c), or to announce and present an enigmatic dish, the *mūma* (14.658e). If it is true that the guests will reproach each other for their voracity, on the whole, table manners do not receive much attention. One should note, however, the vivid description of an Epicurean who throws himself on an eel, removes the flesh from its sides and reduces it to a bone, exclaiming: "Here is the Helen of banquets: I will be its Paris!" (7.298d). To the expert Cynulcus falls the task of attributing to him the prize for gluttony. The act of eating is treated with noteworthy discretion. Eating and speaking at the same time turns out to be problematic, and that problem, which refers to the conventions of the literary genre of the symposium, where dialogue only started once the meal was finished, constitutes one of the dialogue's comic resources. In return, the deipnosophists drink and speak together during the symposium, and Cynulcus, in fact, is half asleep and in a state of drunkenness, a state which his companions take advantage of in order to rub him with perfume (15.685f, 686c).

It is opportune at this point to clarify an ambiguous point in Athenaeus' text that has generated some perplexity in modern commentaries. If at the macro-structural level Athenaeus recounts the unfolding of a banquet and a symposium, from the *apéritif* to the final libation, in the detail of his account he refers without any doubt to several banquets, either to underline their general characteristics, or to bring to the fore a particular fact or event that occurs at a given moment. For example, on a winter day, pumpkin is served to the deipnosophists, who are amazed to find it is fresh (9.372b). Another time, a big fish is served in a vinegar-and-brine-based sauce (9.385b). The reader cannot help but note the multiple indices of this oscillation between one and many: temporal markers ("one day", "often", "every time"),[2] the alternate use of singular and plural ("our symposium", "our symposia").[3]

Athenaeus is sometimes even more explicit. After recalling the conversation on riddles, he interrupts his account to Timocrates, since in the meantime night has fallen, and puts off to the next day the account relating to the wine-cups (10.459b).[4] A similar interruption occurs in the course of the banquet itself: at the beginning of Book 11, the deipnosophists meet at the usual time (*kath'hōran*) and sit rather than lie before the conversation begins. Is it a different banquet, or simply a pause between *deipnon* and *sumposion*, a pause during which the guests had left their couches? In any case, Ulpian, the symposiarch, invites everyone to lie down without wasting any more time, to listen to Plutarch of Alexandria speak of the wine-cups (460a–b and 461e). In the same way, the meeting is interrupted at the end of Book 14, "because it is night now" (664f): it is unclear whether this refers to the symposium or to the dialogue between Athenaeus and Timocrates? In any case, the mention of that interruption brings Book 14 to an end.

Those multiple contextual and temporal markers have sometimes been seen as proof that the entire text of the *Deipnosophists* in its present state is a compendium of the original work; Athenaeus' thirty books would, in that case, have been reduced to fifteen by a compiler who left some indications of how the work was previously organized.[5] The work that we read today, however, was evidently structured from the start in a total of fifteen books, as the beginning and the end of each of those testify.[6] On the basis of those indications we would prefer to draw two different conclusions. First of all, Larensius' circle met regularly, perhaps at times that were agreed in advance (*kath'hōran*). The

---

[2] See e.g. 8.331b–c; 9.385b; 402c: "often kid was served, prepared in various ways"; see also 14.616e, 617f; 15.665a–b.

[3] See e.g. 1.2a: "meeting" (*sunousia*); 1.4b: Larensius' "banquet" (*deipnon*); 15.665a: "these banquets".

[4] With Rodríguez-Noriega Guillén 2000:250–52, I understand this passage as a reference to the time of the frame narrative (Athenaeus recounting the banquets to Timocrates), which explains the use of the present, and not as referring to the time of the events described within that frame (that is, the banquet itself).

[5] K. Mengis, in the footsteps of Kaibel, was one of the principal proponents of this thesis, going so far as to suggest the hypothesis that each of the thirty original books corresponded to a separate banquet, on the model of Plutarch's *Symposiacs*: see Mengis 1920:4ff.

[6] This has been demonstrated by Düring 1936. See also the discussions by Arnott 2000:42ff. and Rodríguez-Noriega Guillén 2000:244–55.

festivities of the table provided the frame for a social and intellectual activity that, in Rome, was known to everyone (1.2a: *poluthruletos*). Secondly, Athenaeus attempts to synthesize important facts and discussions that took place in the course of the many meetings of their circle; for that reason, one can easily admit that extra memories ("one day", *pote*) were inserted in the connecting thread that is the main banquet, which is even more a narrative structure than the faithful account of a given and unique event. The inconsistencies that strike us reveal a text that is in the making, a great enterprise that by its very nature was perhaps bound to remain unfinished, to go through perpetual processes of expansion and reworking.

Thus, in the ritualized stages of their development, the banquet and the *sumposion* offer a familiar connecting thread to help the reader move and orient himself in the labyrinth of words and quotations. Moreover, this connecting thread offers a point of reference to the reader, who can thus follow the distribution of topics within the fifteen books according to the development of a typical banquet. Before closing this section, I would like to underline the crucial role played by the service of the meal's courses, which simultaneously circulates the meal's dishes and the quotations that gloss them. It is the same verb, *paratithesthai*, that describes the presentation of the dishes and the quotation of the texts: a single act of exhibition for both.[7] And the *pinakes*—the trays— that go round abundantly in the course of the banquet and of the conversations that accompany it, carry not only the dishes of the meal, but also their names and the list of literary texts that mention them. The *pinakes* circulating among the guests resonate with Callimachus' *Pinakes*, that monument of Alexandrian bibliography[8]. The unfolding of the banquet is thus the organizational principle of the text. The cooks and the servants, the scholars, ultimately fulfill the same task: to parade the dishes and the words, in an uninterrupted sequence, to everyone's pleasure.

---

[7] *Paratithesthai* in the sense of "to quote"; see e.g. 2.60d–e; 3.76a, 84c, 127b; 4.170e, 6.269e; 7.304b, 317a; 9.387d; 10.423f; 11.467e, 472e, 479c, 485d–f, 501e; 12.525e; 14.629a; 15.676d, 679b, 692f; in the sense of "serving dishes": 1.7d, 8f, 9a; 2.59f, 69c,70f, 90b; 3.100d, 120c–d; 4.130f, 131a, 132a, 136c, etc.

[8] Blum 1991.

11

How to Speak at Table?

"**A**LL THAT IS SAID in Homer is not always said by Homer" (5.178d). This critical insight, which explains the polyphony of the voices and the instances of enunciation in the epic, could be applied to Athenaeus himself: all that is said in Athenaeus is not always said by Athenaeus. First of all because he has chosen the formal and dramatic frame of the dialogue, and thus an interaction between characters who represent different points of view according to their temperament or their professional specialization. And the dialogue does not only give form to the mass of facts, words, and quotations; it also deploys a space of confrontation, criticism, and collective research, which involves everyone's collaboration.

However, there is also another reason why all that is said in Athenaeus is not always said by Athenaeus: the characters of his dialogue spend most of their time quoting written texts—words, sentences, and entire passages. They lend their voices to the silence of the written texts, as was usual, after all, for ancient readers, and one of the dimensions of their game consists in giving to this literary and fragmented speech the continuity, liveliness, and freedom of tone of a conversation in a live situation of verbal exchange. The result is a coded dialogue, regulated by a series of rules and constraints, which draws multiple and sophisticated effects of meaning out of a virtuoso game of decontextualization and recontextualization, of effects of form and prosody created by the mixing of dialects, metrical structures, literary genres, levels of discourse, and forms of knowledge. The dialogue between excerpts from books thus slides into the dialogue of the deipnosophists, creating an aesthetics of discontinuity and diversity, of *poikilia*, and a specific intellectual and discursive space, within which Larensius' library appears as a network of connections between textual loci—a hypertext—rather than a juxtaposition of discrete works rolled and ordered on their shelves.

But before entering Athenaeus' web, let us turn to those who weave its threads, the members of Larensius' circle. To suggest an idea that springs to mind: we are in a register of double theatricality. First of all, theatricality in the dialogue, with its leading duet, Ulpian and Cynulcus, but also with its second-rate and token roles (sophists, cooks, and servants), who all draw on the liveliness of comedy. There is also the theatricality of the process itself, seeing that we are here in the domain of performance, with its vocal registers, pathos, and gestures. The game is even more subtle and reflexive, since Athenaeus' guests amply cite comedy dialogues and lend their own voices to different characters, who in turn introduce a new level of points of view, enunciations, and linguistic registers.[1] This vocal and performative dimension, of the order of *hupokrinesthai*, is essential in the *Deipnosophists*: it creates *poikilia* in linguistic registers and in stylistic forms of expression, and also in the subjects addressed in the course of the conversations.

The *Art of Grammar* by Dionysius Thrax (2nd century BC) and its scholia offer a fascinating insight into the various visual, intellectual, vocal, and performative processes implied by reading a written text.[2] Such an exercise was merciless, and anyone reading aloud a text revealed immediately his training and his culture or his complete lack of competence. Reading aloud a text written in *scriptio continua* meant being able to separate words and to articulate them in meaningful sentences, being able to vocally mark accents, the *tonoi*, the *chronoi*, and the *pneumata*, as well as the prosodic structure and melodic lines of poems. Poetical and dramatic texts were expected to be read according to precise cultural conventions: one should adopt a heroic tone in order to imitate tragic heroes, a lively tone for comic characters from the daily life, a high-pitched voice for elegiac poems, a melodic line while reading lyrical poetry with musical accompaniment. The pitch and tone of the voice should go along with appropriate gestures. The reading of poetry was ordered by sophisticated codes that were taught by grammarians, while rhetors were in charge of the reading of prose. Such cultural rules certainly apply to the recitations and quotations of Larensius' guests, who were displaying not only their memory, but also their culture, their *paideia*, their expert skill in using the most precise vocal techniques in their game of reviving ancient Greek literature. Literary and scholarly performance is a key element in their dialogues.

Athenaeus' characters talk and listen to each other while lying on the banquet's couches (2.47e). By giving preference to conversation over other distractions of the banquet, even with respect to the dining itself, the guests inscribe themselves within the Platonic tradition. Besides, the reproach is made to Cynulcus that he subverts that model and takes the role of the pipe-players

---

[1] See the observations of Wilkins 2000c:32ff.
[2] Ed. Lallot 1998.

and dancers: like them, he disturbs, or even interrupts, the flow of the conversation, the only entertainment that holds pride of place within the frame of a literary banquet (3.97b–c).

Words circulate among the guests like wine-cups (1.1f–2a). They circulate in the unraveling of a series of interventions, be they long or short: everyone takes his turn in the dialogue, some are star-interlocutors, others are more discreet, like the grammarian Leonidas. He takes advantage, for example, of a pause made by Ulpian in order to speak: "It is fair that I should speak, since I have remained silent for so long" (9.367d–e). It is true that for guests to speak presupposes that the others remain silent, that is, that they are a group of listeners.[3] Even the sophist cook, who interrupts Ulpian's learned dissertation to announce the arrival of the *mūma*, enjoys general silence as he undertakes a brilliant encomium of his art, recalling, to begin, that even Cadmus, Dionysus' grandfather, was a *mageiros* (14.658e). That ring of listeners sometimes expresses its approval, its admiration, and its pleasure, applauding the orator for his eloquence, his memory, and his erudition. Plutarch of Alexandria largely deserved that applause for having completed the long alphabetical list of wine-cups (11.503f). Cynulcus, on the contrary, receives no applause after his digression on lentil soup and wealth, which makes him angry, or at least he pretends to be angry (4.159e): "Chair of the banquet, they are not yet hungry, because they are busy with their river of words, and yet they taunt me about what I said concerning lentils... Seeing that, as I was saying, those pundits hate lentils for those reasons, have at least some bread brought to us; there is no need for anything in particular, but if you have some of those celebrated lentils or that soup called 'conchos'." This time, Cynulcus triggers off the group's laughter. After his severe lecture against Plato, Masurius commands everyone's admiration for his *sophia* (5.221a). It then falls to the symposiarch Ulpian to make sure that silence does not descend upon the guests who are petrified as if under the effect of Gorgons, and that the conversation starts again; perhaps by taking the Gorgons as its subject (5.221a–b).

Beginning to speak at the very moment when someone else stops is a way of bringing one's own contribution into the smooth unfolding of the symposium and of the conversation that takes place there. Thus Masurius speaks once Cynulcus is finished speaking: "but since there are still some points left to deal with in our discussion on slaves, I shall contribute too with a song to love in honor of our wise and very dear Democritus" (6.271b). At times the orator might be interrupted in case his words raise an unexpected problem. During

---

3 See what is said at 7.308d: the silence of the Molossus dogs—that is, the Cynics—while it has nothing Pythagorean in itself, makes it possible to move on with the list of fish.

Myrtilus' exposition of his long catalogue of women, at the moment when he mentions Tigris of Leucadia, Pyrrhus' lover, Ulpian, as if Hermes in person had made that problem rise before him (*hermaion ti*), "asked if we knew of the word 'tiger' employed in the masculine." Indeed, in his *Neaera*, Philemon mentions a "tigress": Myrtilus provides the requested occurrence, quoting three verses by Alexis (13.590a–b). When one of the guests does not know how to answer a question, another guest takes his place to avoid falling into silence. When asked by Cynulcus about the use of willows to weave crowns, Ulpian remains silent pretending he is thinking about it, and the question is answered by Democritus (15.671d–f). A little further, it is Democritus who finds himself in difficulty: "In which author is the word 'pistachio' found?" Ulpian asks him. Democritus remains silent, despite the prize of a cup of wine promised by the symposiarch. "Since you don't know what to say, I shall proceed to instruct you, Nicander of Colophon names pistachios in his *Theriaca*, where he says [...]." Ulpian then receives compliments for his brilliant exposition on pistachios (14.649c–e).

The conversation often takes on the playful tone of a game of questions and answers, a game that depending on the case can produce reward or punishment. Ulpian thus orders that Cynulcus should be excluded from the banquet and that he should be covered with "haphazardly woven crowns" (*khudaioi*), but it is only a joke, and he cannot resist the pleasure of quoting what Alexis has to say on those crowns. Ulpian himself excites his companions' curiosity by mentioning a *panēguris* in Eleusis called *Ballētus* (the throwing of stones), about which he will not talk if he does not receive payment (*misthos*) from each of his listeners (9.406d). Similarly, Cynulcus refuses to answer one of Ulpian's questions unless he receives a suitable *misthos* in advance (15.671c). Elsewhere, he settles for the promise of Ulpian's gratitude (*kharis*) in order to instruct him on the feast of the *Phagēsia* (7.275e). Ulpian promises. Fair revenge, since previously, during the meal, Ulpian had threatened to give Cynulcus a sound beating if he did not cite a literary source for the word *koiliodaimōn* ("he who makes a god of his own belly"). As the cynic fell silent, Ulpian gave the answer repeating his threat (3.100b).

It would no doubt be interesting to examine in detail the play of attitudes and gazes, but also the speech registers, since the rhetorical dimension is essential to Athenaeus' text. For example, after a brilliant exposition on pistachios, Ulpian looks at the circle of his listeners, who congratulate him, before resuming: "so that you can admire me for my erudition" (14.649e). This circular gaze (*periblepsas*) applies to an orator looking at his audience, such as Athenion, as he prepares to give his speech to the Athenians in front of the Stoa of Attalus (5.212f). The deipnosophists are men of words, both oral and written. They sometimes raise their voice, using a rhetorical technique learned at school, in particular that of epideictic eloquence, which was in vogue in that period, the Second Sophistic, when both the stars of the genre and the most obscure practitioners of the profession performed in public recitations in the cities of the Greek-speaking regions of the empire.[4] A mix of theatricality and erudition, where culture exhibits itself in highly virtuoso oratory and in the use of *paideia* commonplaces. In Athenaeus we can discover multiple signs of that, for example in the passage in which he underlines the well-oiled mechanics (*trokhilia*, in its primary sense a "machine to lift heavy loads"; LSJ has "block-and-tackle equipment, pulley") of Myrtilus' speech on famous *hetairai* (13.587f).

Here, in fact, lies the deep ambiguity of the meetings of Larensius' circle: are they oratory performances or banquets? Are we in the public space of the agora, of a theater or of a lecture hall, where sophists liked to speak, or in the private space of a Roman house, where a banquet and a symposium are taking place? Such is the question asked by Cynulcus (6.270d): "If I had been invited here only to listen to lectures (*eis akroāseis logōn*), I would have taken care to come when the forum was full (that is how one of the sophists used to define the hour of public declamations (*deixeis*), and for that reason the common people called him "Plethagoras"). But if we have bathed in order to dine on trivial words, 'the contribution is too high for me, a listener', to quote Menander. For that reason, glutton, I let you stuff yourself with food like this." And he pretends to get up and depart.

To use the title of a theatrical play by Victor Hugo, the great question that runs through the first ten books of the *Deipnosophists* is "Mangeront-ils ?" ("Will they manage to eat?"). Certainly as far as the wine is concerned, in the following five books the cups circulate and are generously filled and emptied, and besides, the tradition of symposium dialogues made it possible to drink and converse at the same time.[5] A quote from Alexis recalls this point precisely at the right moment: wine "turns into *philologoi* all those who drink it in good quantity" (2.39b). But is it possible to speak, and to be listened to, while eating?

Everything works as if eating and speaking about food were two incompatible activities, unless they merge into a form of "mastication of the word". The dishes of the banquet are served to be quoted (*paratithesthai*), and the trays

---

[4]   Some standard works (among the immense literature) on the subject, which are useful for situating Athenaeus within his cultural and rhetorical universe: Bompaire 1958; Bowersock 1969; Pernot 1993 (Pernot's work allows us, for example, to situate Cynulcus' tirade on lentils within the tradition of paradoxical praise: see pp. 532–46, and especially p. 540 n.254); Anderson 1993; Schmitz 1997. See also the stimulating synthesis of Anderson 1974, where the accent is put on the performative dimension of the virtuoso *recitals* of the deipnosophists.

[5]   See however 10.448b, where Aemilianus launches the discussion on riddles "in such a way as to put some distance between us and our cups."

(*pinakes*) that carry the courses thus become bibliographical and lexical tables. The conversation presupposes the presence of the dishes, but these are objects of reflection, gazing, and desire, and in the distance created by unsatisfied gluttony, or even hunger, a space is found for the recollection of words and texts, for the discourse on food and cooking. Ulpian, a fanatic of the *zētēsis*, always asks his questions in relation to the dishes before the first mouthful has been taken (1.1d–e). And during the banquet, those two temporal dimensions, that of the food and that of the conversation, are continuously in conflict, both being dependent on the rhythm of the service. "Come on, my dear friends, in which author do we find the term *mētra* (sow's womb)? We have sufficiently filled our stomachs and it is time now to talk again," says Ulpian (3.96e–f). When the guests stretch out their hands towards the bread, it is Galen who cuts in: "We shall not eat until you have heard also from me what has been said on bread and muffins and also on flour by the sons of Asclepius" (3.115c). After Galen's report, they finally decide to eat, and a starter of salted fish is served. But will they really eat? Leonidas launches the discussion on salted fish (3.116a), in the course of which the physician Dionysocles (116d), Daphnus of Ephesus (116f), Varus (118d), Ulpian (118f), Plutarch (119a), and Myrtilus (119b) speak after him. At least, one learns at the end that the sophists really eat their salted fish (120b). And when, after interminable lists and speeches on fish, the deipnosophists finally prepare to eat, it is once again a physician, Daphnus, who requests the beginning of the meal to be delayed: the question of fish is not yet closed, since the physicians have not all spoken about it (8.355a).

The desire to know, curiosity, the expectation to find a solution to a lexical problem: all this stifles the appetite. "I shall not eat until you tell me in which authors this wheat porridge is mentioned," says Ulpian. Aemilianus replies, "I shall first of all talk to you about the wheat porridge by citing [serving? *paratithemenos*] these verses from Antiphanes' *Anthea*" (3.127a-b). And when Cynulcus asks Ulpian about the feast of the Phagesia, the latter, puzzled, has the banquet's service interrupted, although it was already the evening. He invites Cynulcus to give the answer himself, "so that you may enjoy your meal even more" (7.275c). At a certain point, it becomes necessary to ask the cooks to take the necessary precautions so that the long feast of words can take place without having to serve dishes that have already become cold long ago (8.354 d).

Cynulcus does not tolerate very well the interruptions, and the delays, the length of some speeches, which constrain the audience to a ritual fast, where they wait for the end of the discourse like others wait for a star to rise (4.156a–b). At the end of Democritus' long speech on slavery, as we have seen, Cynulcus exclaims: "But I am still very hungry ... because I have ingested nothing but words. So now let us stop once and for all this interminable chitchat and let us take some of this food" (6.270b). And another cynic, in the heart of the discussions on fish, thinks he has fallen in the midst of the feast of the Thesmophoriae, "seeing that we are starved like mullets" (7.307f). Myrtilus answers, "You shall not touch the food until you [the Cynics], or your co-disciple Ulpian, will have explained why mullet is the only fish to be called *nēstis*, 'empty belly'" (308a). There is great irony, of course, in the words and the quotations, which rebound like balls.

Even as the group is finally coming close to the end of the dinner, Ulpian remains intransigent. He is lying on a symposium couch alone—his companions are perhaps tired of his obsession—eating little, observing the other guests, and tirelessly asking fundamental questions: "What is vinegar sauce?" (9.385c). On the day when a big fish is served in a sauce of vinegar and brine, Ulpian, that collector of thorns, asks: "Where do we find vinegar-and-brine sauce attested?" But this time the greatest part of the guests damns him to hell and begins eating without answering him. Furthermore, and quite to the point, Cynulcus adds a quote from Metagenes: "But, my dear, first we eat, then ask me whatever you like; now I am really hungry and, in a way, without memory" (9.385b–c). The hungry stomach has neither ears nor memory. Only Myrtilus sides with Ulpian: do not touch the food but go on chattering without pause. Besides, that was the indispensable condition if Athenaeus' work was to proceed to the fifteenth book.

The speeches of the deipnosophists stand thus in a paradoxical relationship with their very argument. Speaking of food means setting up a relation of homology between speech and food, a relation of mimesis. Athenaeus' table talk is like the fulfillment of a gourmet tasting session: words are savored as dishes would be savored.[6] Thus to speak of fish is to "ichthyologize" (7.308d; 8.360d). To speak of figs is to "sycologize" (3.79a), to speak of wine is to "oenologize" (2.40f) and to avidly devour the names of wines (ibid.; *laphussein* is a very strong verb, employed for dogs, lions, or birds of prey). "Having at the tip of one's tongue" Sicily's moray eel, other eels, the intestines of the Pachinian tuna, the kids of Melos, and more, means to master the gastronomical *topoi* and to be capable of making them slip into the banquet's conversation, like that Carmus of Syracuse who before going to dinner filled his memory with quotations (1.4a–d). "I beg you," says Ulpian, "not to deny me an explanation of what 'bull water' is; I am thirsty for such expressions." Cynulcus replied: "I then drink with you—he said—the cup of friendship, since you are thirsty for words" (3.122e–f).

---

6   From this point of view, Athenaeus occupies the founding position within a long tradition. See Jeanneret 1986.

Even Larensius follows Ulpian's model and proposes a question to the company, "since we feed ourselves with inquiries" (9.398b).

Of course, those continually interrupted banquets, those dishes that become cold during the long and learned disquisitions, contribute in scattering comic scenes across the text.[7] In the same way as the dinners of comedy, Larensius' guests like the "meals about which the comic poets speak: rather than constitute a delicacy for the palate, they procure great pleasure to the listener" (9.402d). At least, that is how it is for the reader. Yet one cannot but see even in that game the signs of a tension: Athenaeus makes problematic his transgression of one of the traditional rules of the literary genre of the symposium, where one eats in silence and then converses while drinking wine. To eat and to speak at the same time, to speak of food and cuisine at table, is a paradoxical project that is inserted between the two antithetical positions of Ulpian and Cynulcus: to speak without eating or to eat without speaking, such is the dilemma that feeds the conversation.[8] What is perhaps at play in the *Deipnosophists* is a conception of pleasure:[9] the notion is explained through philosophical doctrines, illustrated by amusing anecdotes, problematized in the characterization of its deviations and excesses (*truphē, opsophagia*), politicized through the highlighting of its links with the Hellenistic monarchies. But what sort of pleasure is pursued within Larensius' circle? There is a form of distance and restraint in respect to a social entertainment, the symposium, which offers a structuring frame, a field of investigation, regularly mediated through language, memory, words, and books. Larensius' banquet is at the same time a social ritual and a laboratory in which objects, dishes, gestures, and words are observed with an attitude of critical distance and with the help of sophisticated apparatus. In Larensius' house, the dining-room is indistinguishable from the library.

The reader will have understood: Larensius' feasts are not the *Cena Trimalchionis*: there are no baroque excesses, save in the field of language and erudition. The long procession of famous *hetairai* does not bring with it the pleasures of Eros. The buffoons and other shows introduced by Larensius do not introduce comic interludes: they are nothing more than subjects of conversation, where laughter is provoked by quotations, and not by the entertainment itself (14.613c–d). The flute-players and the crowns, the wine and the *skolia*, are not a prelude to a *kōmos*—at best they cause Cynulcus' light drunkenness.

---

[7]   See e.g. 14.649a: "'You have your *koptē*, Ulpian, my good accountant of words, and I advise you to devour it (*apeshiein*)'. And without wasting any time, he took it and began to eat it. Everyone burst out laughing, and Democritus added: 'I did not ask you to eat it, my dear word-hunter, but not to eat it; indeed, in his *Phineus*, the comic Theopompus used *apesthiein* in this sense...'" The only time when Ulpian eats with appetite, he is caught in the trap of the meaning of words.

[8]   See the observations by Wilkins 2000c:26–28.

[9]   My reflection is inspired by Romeri 2000.

12

Libraries and Bibliophiles

THE MENTION OF Larensius' rich library at the beginning of Book I does not fill out the portrait of the host of the banquets, a rich Roman bibliophile and philhellene. The library also plays an essential role in Athenaeus' work. The link that unites text, banquets, and library is a link of analogy, of condensation, of mirroring, and of structural homology.[1]

Larensius' library has its place in the history of great collections of books in the ancient world; Athenaeus makes it into the present culmination of a line that originated with the "libraries" of Polycrates of Samos, Peisistratus and Euclid in Athens, Nicostratus of Cyprus, and that had subsequently passed through Aristotle's Lyceum, Alexandria, and Pergamon (1.3a–b).[2] Such a genealogy thus brings us from Athens to Rome through Alexandria and Pergamon; from the libraries of cities, philosophical schools, and Hellenistic kingdoms, to the private library of an imperial high official. Athenaeus tells us nothing of the public libraries founded in Rome since the initiative of Asinius Pollio in 39 BC, arising out of the inspiration of Julius Caesar. And in that version of his text (admittedly abbreviated), the author does not even mention the role played by the great private libraries in the spread of the Greek literary and philosophical heritage in Italy from the time of the victorious generals of the Republic.[3] Larensius' library however, by virtue of its very existence, is the sign that the Urbs was now one of the sites where the intellectual heritage of Hellenism was concentrated.

Larensius' love of books is not an isolated case. If the correspondence between Cicero and Atticus documents how it was possible to build up a good

---

[1] For an earlier discussion of my thoughts on this question see Jacob 2000.
[2] Here Athenaeus' inspiration is a reconstruction of the history of libraries that can be found in many other authors of the imperial period. Aulus Gellius, *Attic Nights* 7.17.1–2; Isidorus of Seville, *Etymologies* 6.3.3–5; Tertullian, *Apology* 18.5. Those authors may all refer to the same source (perhaps Varro's *On Libraries*?). On this tradition see Canfora 1990 and Jacob 2000.
[3] On the history of libraries in Rome see Langie 1908; Wendel 1955; Fedeli 1986; Blank 1992:152–78; and Pesando 1994.

library of Greek texts at the end of the Republic,[4] imperial literature also presents us with some noteworthy examples of book collectors, ridiculous ones like Trimalchio or the "bibliomaniacs" mocked by Seneca and Lucian,[5] or exemplary like Pliny the Younger and Pliny the Elder.[6] A chapter of Vitruvius' *De Architectura* shows how the location of the library was one of the preoccupations of those who dealt with the building of houses (6.7). Some of Larensius' and Athenaeus' contemporaries in Rome were famous for their libraries: that of Serenus Sammonicus, a member of Iulia Domna's circle, contained 62,000 rolls, at least in the form in which his son transmitted it to the emperor Gordian II.[7] The physician Galen, one of Athenaeus' characters, also owned an imposing collection of books, which went up in flames, together with other libraries in the Forum and Palatine areas during the fire of AD 192.

Athenaeus insists that it is the ancient Greek books that bring glory to Larensius. This does not preclude his owning a collection of Latin texts distinct from the Greek ones, as was the habit in Rome both in private collections and in public institutions.[8] Those private libraries could be open to a circle of people who were friends or had intellectual connections with the owner. In the first century BC Philodemus' library at Herculaneum and Lucullus' at Tusculum provide the best examples for the pre-imperial period.[9] The lending or exchange of books, and the cultured conversations that were devoted to them, could be the focus of a social life that also included the pleasures of the table: thus Seneca sharply criticizes the presence of big libraries in the dining rooms of the Roman houses of his time, which had no other reason to exist than to give the appearance of their owner's high culture.[10] However, the links between library and dining room are not totally arbitrary: even in the Museum of Alexandria,

---

[4] See Cicero, *Letters to Atticus* 1.7; 1.10.4; 1.20.7; 2.6.1; 4.4.1; 4.5.4; 4.8.2; see also *Tusculan Disputations* 2.9; 3.7; *Letters to his Friends* 16.20.

[5] Petronius, *Satyricon* 48.4; Seneca, *On Tranquility of Mind* 9.4–7; Lucian, *The Ignorant Book-Collector*.

[6] Pliny the Younger, *Letters* 1.8; 2.17.

[7] *Scriptores Historiae Augustae, Gordianus* 18.2. According to the *Suda* (s.v. "Epaphroditus"), Nero's freedman, who was also Epictetus' master, owned a personal library of 30,000 books. See also Isidore of Seville, *Etymologies* 6.6 on the library of Pamphilus of Caesarea, which also contained ca. 30,000 volumes (3rd century AD). We have no way of verifying those numbers, but it is nevertheless interesting to compare them to the ones we have for the library of the Serapaeum of Alexandria: 42,800 rolls according to Tzetzes, *Prolegomena On Comedy* 32 (ed. Koster).

[8] See Cicero, *Letters to His Brother Quintus* 3.4.5; Petronius, *Satyricon* 48.4; Sidonius Apollinaris, *Letters* 4.11.6; Suetonius, *Lives of the Caesars* 44; Isidore of Seville, *Etymologies* 6.5.2. Athenaeus cites only three Latin works: 4.160c (Varro and Roman grammarians); 4.168e (the *History of Rome* by P. Rutilius Rufus, which was, however, written in Greek); 6.273b (Cotta's treatise on the Roman constitution). See Zecchini 1989:236–39.

[9] Plutarch, *Life of Lucullus* 42; see also Cicero, *On Moral Ends* 3.7–8.

[10] Seneca, *On Tranquility of Mind* 9.5.

where the famous library was lodged, scholars took their meals in common,[11] perpetuating a model known from the Athenian philosophical schools, for example Aristotle's Lyceum.[12]. Moreover, it seems that the library in Pergamon, which may have imitated the organization of that at Alexandria, also included a symposium hall, within the sanctuary of Athena Polias.[13] In his lively account of a banquet offered by Herodes Atticus in a villa at Cephisia, Aulus Gellius mentions how the famous professor asked for the first volume of Epictetus' *Discourses*, as edited by Arrian, and how an extract was read aloud, in order to give a lecture to a young, braggart Stoic philosopher (*Attic Nights*, 1.2.6–7): here again, there is a proximity between the dining room and the library, between symposium conversation and books.

The library plays a central role in Larensius' circle and in the text of Athenaeus, even if we have no indication as to its placement within the *domus*, to its personnel of slaves and freedmen, or to the role played in it by Athenaeus himself. However, all of Larensius' guests share a substantial interest in ancient Greek books, and their meeting evokes the characteristics of a reading club for bibliophiles. Larensius' library was open to the members of that circle, and one can imagine a game of exchanges and lending of books, as well as the tireless search for rarer works.[14] For example, in Book 13, Larensius admits he has not yet succeeded in putting his hands on the work of Hieronymus of Rhodes that cites a decree on women, but promises his interlocutor to send him the book as soon as he has managed to find it (556b).

Of course, all the deipnosophists have their own personal library, even if such libraries were perhaps less impressive than that of their Roman patron. Cynulcus, for example, after having embarrassed Ulpian with a question on the feast of the *Phagēsia*, gives him the answer citing Clearchus of Soli's treatise *On Riddles* from memory and concludes: "And if you don't believe me, my companion, since the book is in my possession, I shall not deny it to you" (7.276a). Larensius could immediately have taken the rolls[15] in his library, seeing that he shows familiarity with the work of Clearchus, indispensible reading for

---

[11] Strabo, *Geography* 17.1.8.C.793–94. One should also recall in Athenaeus the description of the ship of Hiero of Syracuse, the *Alexandris*, with its study room (*scholastērion*) furnished with a library and five couches (5.207e–f).

[12] The will of the scholarch Strato leaves the library as inheritance to his successor (with the exception of the books he had written himself), as well as all the tableware necessary for meals in common, the couches, and the drinking cups (Diogenes Laertius, *Lives of the Eminent Philosophers* 5.62).

[13] Callmer 1944:151.

[14] As has been highlighted by Anderson 1974:2174–76, Athenaeus' scholarly erudition goes well beyond the corpus of classical authors read and studied in the schools of the Second Sophistic.

[15] The work probably contained more than one, since Athenaeus refers to the first: 14.620c. See fr. 64 and 91 (Wehrli).

whoever wanted to perpetuate the tradition of classical symposia and their social games (10.448c).

The contribution made by those scholars to the banquet takes the form of *grammata*, books taken out of their linen or leather bags. The term *strōmatodesmos* (or *strōmatodesmon*) describes, in its primary sense, what contained the necessary gear for the couch; the sack had to have a certain capacity, since Cleopatra hid in one of them to penetrate unnoticed into the palace of Alexandria and meet Caesar.[16] We must therefore imagine our deipnosophists arriving at Larensius' not with a simple bookcase (*capsa* or *scrinium*), but with sacks full of papyrus rolls, necessary to the smooth progress of their meetings. The best tribute they could pay to their host was to make him discover books that he did not yet know. That seems to be the key to understanding those patrons who were learned and gourmets at the same time: Larensius turns his Roman table into Cockaigne (or Lusitania: 8.331b–c), while his guests restrict themselves to bringing their own *logaria*, their small speeches, and the books on which they are based. Indeed, it is precisely from the books that they extract the materials with which they contribute to the banquet, for example to the discussion on fish (7.277b–c).[17] Even the sparkling conversation and the flowering of quotations that it generates participate in that spirit of interchange (see 3.96d; 6.271b; 15.692d).

Our sophists are all on the lookout for rare books. Ulpian, the word-hunter, devotes himself to his favorite activity in every place: in the street, in the baths, and in bookshops (1.1d–e). One can also suppose that his companions also frequented Rome's bookshops and libraries: "From which library, O most erudite grammarians, came those most venerable authors, Chrysippus and Harpocration, who slandered the names of noble philosophers by virtue of their homonymy?" asks Ulpian (14.648c). And it is with his pornographic library under his arm that Myrtilus is depicted by Cynulcus while he makes incursions into taverns and inns in gallant company: it is nevertheless true that among those nefarious books we find Aristophanes of Byzantium, Apollodorus and Gorgias of Athens, Ammonius and Antiphanes, who are all recognised sources on Athenian prostitutes (13.567a).

Aulus Gellius' *Attic Nights* allow us to complete the picture traced by Athenaeus, assuming that between the reigns of Antoninus and Hadrian on the one hand, and those of Marcus Aurelius, Commodus, and Severus on the other,

---

[16] Plutarch, *Life of Julius Caesar* 49.

[17] See 13.555a, where a quotation from Antiphanes mentions banquets in which everyone brought their part, and where blows were given and received for a prostitute; 13.572c, on the misfortunes of a young man who came to the banquet without any other contribution than himself; 8.362d, on the *eranoi*, those banquets to which the guests contributed by bringing the food; 6.270d, where Cynulcus mentions his contribution.

there was no significant line of discontinuity in the activity of *letterati*. Aulus Gellius' characters also frequent Rome's bookshops, where it might happen that other clients ask for their advice, for example on the authenticity and the edition of a text—the bookseller specializes in ancient books, seeing that in his shop one could find Fabius' *Annals* (5.41). There one meets true and fake scholars, sitting in bookshops, reading out loud and discussing textual criticism and interpretation of difficult texts (13.31; 18.4). One also meets authentic scholars, for whom it is of crucial importance, even at the height of the summer heat, to succeed in finding a treatise by Aristotle, borrowing it from the library of the temple of Hercules of Tivoli (19.5 and 9.14.3). Aulus Gellius and his friends also obviously frequented the great libraries of Rome: the Ulpiana (11.17.1–4), that of the Domus Tiberiana, rebuilt by Domitian (13.20), and that of the Temple of Peace (16.82). Neither do they neglect provincial libraries, like that of Patras, which owned a very ancient copy of the *Odyssey* by Livius Andronicus (18.9.5–6).

This search for books runs through the *Deipnosophists* from top to bottom, and Larensius' guests do not miss a chance to mention the lucky occasions when this or that extremely rare work came into their hands. Such discoveries are shared and transmitted during the table conversations. "I came upon another treatise of Chrysippus of Tyana, entitled *The Book of the Breadmaker*," says Arrian as he begins his list of breads (3.113a). Among the extant *Dinner-Party Letters* of Hippolochus and Lynceus of Samos, Athenaeus had the luck to come upon those by Lynceus describing the feasts of Antigonus and Ptolemy and he wants to share their content with Timocrates: "We shall not give you the letters themselves; but since the one by Hippolochus can only rarely be found, I will describe to you what is written in it, for your delectation and pastime" (4.128a–c). Indeed, our bibliophiles like sharing things, and Athenaeus' text becomes a library of rare texts that are abundantly, if not directly, cited: "Matron the Parodist—says Plutarch—describes with much grace an Attic banquet: considering how rare it is, I shall not hesitate, my friends, to bring this text back to your memory" (4.134d). The same goes for the treatise by Moschion on the amazing boat of Hiero of Syracuse (5.206d).[18] And Democritus of Nicomedia recalls the way in which he acquired in Alexandria the small treatise (*sungrammation*) by Menodotus in which a problem related to one of Anacreon's compositions found its solution (15.673d): a solution that Hephaestion had adopted and published in a treatise which appeared under his name, and which Democritus had later discovered in the shop of a Roman bookseller. Such an expert book collector had no difficulty comparing texts and identifying a plagiarist. The same Democritus also mentions his discovery of a book by Polycharmus of Naucratis with the

[18] See also 15.672a.

title *Aphrodite*, where one could find everything one might wish to know on the "crown of Naucratis" (15.675f).

Larensius could not but enjoy such conversations. As for us, modern readers of Athenaeus, we discover in them an unsuspected library. If we are familiar with Homer, Hesiod, some lyrics, the three great tragedians and Aristophanes, the Attic orators, Plato and Aristotle, some Alexandrians poets, and some imperial prose-writers (among whom Lucian stands out because of his lively wit), Athenaeus brings to the surface a library of forgotten authors: in our vision of Greek literature, we need to find a place for the Archestratus' *Gastrologia* (1.4e, and *passim*), the Hesiod or the Theognis of the gourmets (7.310a); for the *Dinner-Party Letters* of Hippolochus of Macedonia and Lynceus of Samos (4.128a–c); for the treatise of Callixeinus of Rhodes on Alexandria, from which Athenaeus quotes a spectacular description of the parade organized by Ptolemy Philadelphus in Alexandria (5.196a–203e); for the treatise of Herodotus of Lycia *On Figs* (3.75e) or for those of Euthydemus of Athens *On Salted Fish* (3.116a) and *On Vegetables* (3.74b); for that of Harmodius of Lepreon on *Customs and Traditions of Phigaleia* (10.442b) or that of Chameleon of Heraclea *On Drunkenness* (9.461a). These are some titles among many others from the library of Athenaeus, which is also one of our main sources for comic, historical, and lyrical fragments.

Athenaeus, like the characters he stages in his work, shows a special familiarity and care for the book as the frame enclosing a quotation, or as a witness of the use of a word, attributable to an author, identified by a title, and recognizable thanks to some material traits, for example the number of volumes (rolls) that compose it, or its *incipit*. The erudition deployed by Athenaeus in the area of bibliography puts him in a peculiar position among the scholars and compilers of the imperial period. In Aelian, for example, one could search in vain for a similar precision in the description of the books, the control of their titles and their attribution, in the indications that make it possible to identify a copy or a work. Diogenes Laertius is closer to our author, even if his project is entirely different: bibliography appears as an important component of the lives of Greek philosophers. Athenaeus could be compared to Galen too, who provides us with many insights on his library, on the writing and "publishing" of his own treatises, on his methods as commentator of Hippocrates. The recently discovered treatise *Peri Alupias* (*On the Absence of Grief*) offers a lively account of Galen's scholarly activity in Rome, of his unending quest for rare and ancient texts, in the imperial libraries as well in the bookshops. He was able to evaluate the authenticity of texts, checking their titles in the catalogues of the library of Alexandria or making his own judgment on stylistic criteria. He did not hesitate to copy rare texts and he devoted an important part of his time to correcting and editing manuscripts, in order to have a better text: he had his own copies of Aristotle and Theophrastus, of Platonic and Stoic philosophers such as Clitomachus or Chrysippus. He had in his collection a copy of the Aristarchean edition of Homer's epics as well as an edition of Plato established by Panaetius. Galen also produced his own reference books, such as an epitome of Didymus' lexicon of the vocabulary of Attic comedy. He also wrote a synopsis of Plato's dialogues and a lexicon of the Attic words in prose writers and authors of comedies (58 book-rolls). All these precious editions, his personal "work in progress", along with many other personal belongings, were burnt during the AD 192 fire.[19]

Galen's interests and scholarly activity, obviously, were close to those of Ulpian, Cynulcus, and Larensius' other guests. As a commentator, Galen mirrors the practices of an "intensive reader", that is, a reader focusing on few texts, but devoting himself to in-depth interpretation. But he appears too like an "extensive reader", like Athenaeus and his characters, who browsed such a large number of books in their lexicographical and antiquarian quest. Naturally, one cannot assert that Athenaeus had in his hands every book whose "factsheet" he gives or from which he quotes an excerpt; but even if his bibliographical information comes from secondary sources, it is significant that he chose to present it again within his own work.

The bibliographical references are of course essential, when one takes care, like Ulpian, to root words within literary quotations that testify to their usage, form, and meaning. However, Athenaeus' concern goes far beyond the accuracy of the quotations, and shows his expert interest in books, for their history, for all the intellectual problems linked to the verification of their authenticity. A librarian's and a book collector's concern, which could make one think about the involvement of Athenaeus in the organization of Larensius' library, but also about the links between the *Deipnosophists* and that library.

If one accepts at face value the numbers provided by Gulick, Athenaeus cites around 800 authors and 2,500 works; if one takes into account the fact that a great part of those works came in the form of several papyrus rolls (or volumes), the library of Athenaeus undoubtedly represents a considerable collection.[20] By "library of Athenaeus" I do not mean the library of Larensius, nor the one made up of the books that our author was able to consult directly, but the intellectual space deployed by the countless quotations, direct or indirect, contained in his work: those quotations presuppose a stable order, a classification, an organi-

---

[19] Boudon-Millot and Jouanna 2010.
[20] The way books were counted in ancient libraries consisted in calculating the number of rolls, not the number of works. It is certain that a library of 2,500 works, which probably contained works as long as that of Nicholas of Damascus (144 rolls), and several copies of the same texts, could approach the 62,000 "volumes" of Serenus Sammonicus.

zation, that assign to each author a given time and origin, and a place in the typology of knowledge, literary genres, and disciplines.

The insistence of Athenaeus on books, even when he draws nothing else from them than a quotation or some specific piece of information, is omnipresent within the *Deipnosophists*, whether it be a question of testing, or at least suggesting, through concrete details, that the author has really had in hand the books he cites; or a question of providing the readers, who presumably share the same cultural preoccupations as Athenaeus and his characters, a set of objective data that allow them to identify the books cited (for example, in order to acquire them for their library), or to verify that the copy that they own is complete (i.e. that it does not lack a single roll). Neither should we disregard the production of specific meanings within the very dialogue of the deipnosophists: the extent and precision of their quotations throw light on their polymathy and their memory, especially if the quoted book is rare, or if the quotation of it offers a paradoxical view. The precise, verifiable bibliographical reference, on the other hand, also serves to verify authenticity within that polyphonic archaeology of Greek language and customs.

The bibliographical information, understood in the broad sense as everything that will contribute to defining the origin of a quotation and the status of the author from whom it comes, thus acquires a certain autonomy in relation to the actual development of the conversation. Digressive by nature, it creates an autonomous level of knowledge. For example, when he has in mind to introduce a quotation from Aristophanes' *Wealth* concerning plates of fish that turn into silver plates in the presence of divinity, Athenaeus provides the following information: "Aristophanes the comic, who according to Heliodorus of Athens in his treatise on *The Acropolis*, which is made up of fifteen books, was from Naucratis" (6.229d–e). The reader is provided with five items: the mention of a literary genre that helps identifying Aristophanes, a secondary source, Heliodorus of Athens, the title of his work, the number of rolls it encompasses, and last, a surprising mention of Aristophanes' homeland, Naucratis, based on Heliodorus' authority. Such a smattering of information shows the erudition of Athenaeus as well as his interest for everything related to his own homeland, Naucratis. Moreover, mentioning the number of rolls of some particularly voluminous works fits well too with the syndrome of collection and accumulation that characterizes the *Deipnosophists*, but it is also a way of underlining the breadth of reading of Athenaeus and his characters, and the wealth of their libraries: citing Book 116 of the *Histories* by Nicholas of Damascus, Athenaeus notes that this *polubiblos* work contained a hundred and forty four books (6.249a).[21] The

---

[21] See also 1.5a–b: "Timalchidas of Rhodes, who wrote a treatise in epic verse in eleven books, or perhaps more" (Athenaeus refers only to Books 4 and 9). Is it because he suspects that the

standard form of quotation, however, contains at least three items: the name of the author (with complementary elements of identification like the ethnonym or the literary category), the title of the work, and the volume in the case of works that were made up of multiple volumes.[22] Of the twelve quotations from Nicholas of Damascus, eight indicate the volume they come from: those references show that the quotations chosen by Athenaeus come from Books 103–116, either because he only had access to those fourteen rolls, or because he chose to limit himself to those, using Nicholas of Damascus as the continuator of Poseidonius.[23]

Athenaeus also takes care to mention the edition he cites, in particular for comedies, which were often subject to revision. Consequently he makes clear whether he is citing the first or the second edition of a play,[24] with the term *diaskeue* describing even more precisely a revised edition (10.429e; 14.663c). Athenaeus also knows that two different titles can in reality refer to two editions of the same comedy.[25] Even if he draws those details from an indirect source, Athenaeus nevertheless shows his familiarity with that dramatic corpus and with the bibliographical problems it entails.

Another characteristic of Hellenistic bibliography is the care taken to adduce bibliographic details that will allow the identification of the author among possible homonyms, and also to locate him within the typology of literary genres and intellectual disciplines. "Poseidonius the Stoic" makes it possible to identify with certainty the philosopher and historian used plentifully by Athenaeus, and avoids any confusion with a certain Poseidonius of Corinth (1.13b), author of a versified *Art of Fishing*.[26] Theophrastus of Eresus is presented as the disciple of Aristotle (9.387a), in the same way as Clearchus of Soli (6.234f). Poets are described as authors of epic, dithyrambs, or iambic

---

eleventh book is not the last? Other references in Athenaeus to the total number of rolls in a work: 2.60d–e (Cephisodorus); 6.229e (Heliodorus of Athens); 7.312e (Sostratus); 13.597a (Hermesianax of Colophon); 15.673e (Adrastus).

22 The number of lines of a text (the stichometric indications), while a criterion of identification used in library catalogues, is an instrument of control in the process of copying or editing a text, but is never used as an instrument of internal orientation in a text, and Athenaeus himself does not use that form of localization.

23 As Zecchini 1989:117–20 suggests.

24 4.171c: first edition of Aristophanes' *Clouds*; 7.299b and 8.345f: second edition of the *Clouds*; 9.367f: first edition of Magnes' *Dionysus*; 14.646e: second edition of the *Dionysus*; 6.247a–c: quotation from the two editions of Diphylus' *Synoris*; see also 9.373c (Menander) and 10.413c (Euripides).

25 See 3.110b; 6.247c; 8.358d; 10.429c; 11.496f. See also 9.373f–374e: Athenaeus (or his source) refers to a *pinax* relating to representations of drama where it is highlighted that the comedies of Anaxandrides have been preserved even though they had not been victorious.

26 One should however note the various ways in which Athenaeus refers to the former: "Stoic", "philosopher", of Apamea, of Rhodes, or even "my Poseidonius".

poetry. The comics are placed within the history of the genre.[27] Mnesimachus, for example, is a poet of middle comedy (9.387a), while Sciras, who came from Taranto, belongs to Italic comedy (9.402b). If the quotations are extracted from books, those books in turn find their place in a library whose great subdivisions have been defined and organized by Alexandrian erudition.

That literary erudition also manifests itself in the chronological and historical indications that allow us to situate this or that author. Such indications are few in number.[28] Thus, we learn that Callias of Athens preceded Strattis by little (10.453c), or that Anacreon and Sappho were not contemporaries, contrary to what is stated by Hermesianax (13.599c).

The care put into bibliographic identification sometimes leads Athenaeus to cite the first lines of a text. This indication, typical of the practice of Alexandrian librarians, made it possible to identify short compositions that were part of larger collections and that did not necessarily have individual titles. When he has the idea to cite some verses by Simonides on a memorable goat's cheese, Athenaeus begins by quoting the *archē* of that iambic poem (14.658c), and does the same for a poem by Pindar (*Olympians* 13) and for a *skolion* (13.573f–574a). For an ode of Alcaeus, he indicates the beginning and the end of the composition (3.85f). The same precaution applied to comedies, where homonymous plays and problems of attribution could make the identification of a text difficult (8.342d: Antiphanes' *Citharoede*, which was probably to be distinguished from the *Citharist* by the same author, also quoted by Athenaeus at 15.681c). In the case of Archestratus' work, known under four different titles, and attributed to an author from Syracuse or Gela, only the beginning of the text made a secure identification possible, together with the detail that it is an epic poem (1.4d–e). This bibliographic practice also appears in the case of prose texts, such as a speech by Lysias (5.209f; 13.611e), or the *Hypomnemata* of Hegesander of Delphi (11.479d).

If we can acknowledge that a library constitutes an ordered container, a general space of classification and an ordering of the works of Greek literature within which one could move with the help of the appropriate map (like Callimachus' *Pinakes*), then it becomes crucial to situate every word and quotation in its place, in a determined text, itself integrated in turn within an author's corpus, which belongs to a literary genre, to a philosophical school, or to a specific discursive field. Bibliographical references are instruments of navigation in that common space that is the library of a learned community, namely

---

[27] Athenaeus shows his good knowledge of the Alexandrian scholarship on the comic genre: Lycophron, Eratosthenes, Antiochus of Alexandria.

[28] See also 2.51a, 71a–b; 4.128a, 183e; 5.218b–c; 11.470f; 15.698a.

the totality of known books, accessible or esoteric, present or not in material libraries. They offer stable points of reference, making possible the access to a text or to one of its *loci*, wherever that text may be found.

The abundance of bibliographic indications present in the *Deipnosophists* can be explained by the fact that this ordered container has cracks: the circulation of ancient Greek books, the constitution of Roman private libraries by virtue of acquisitions from unspecified providers, the deviations detected with respect to the great Hellenistic libraries (Alexandria, Pergamon), which still represented the norm. All those factors demanded of bibliophiles increased vigilance, specific research, and at times the realization of the impossibility of determining the author or the title of a work, in particular when indirect sources attribute the same quotation to different books.

Athenaeus takes care to voice his uncertainties, and there are indeed many occasions where he mentions such incidents of tradition: is it a question of damaged rolls? Of lost or inverted titles? Of several copies of a single text under the name of different authors? Or doubts that already appear in the various bibliographical "aids" that were at the disposal of the author? Or confusions created by the indirect sources and the lexica used by Athenaeus? Three authors, for example, are indicated for the *Treatise on Agriculture* from which Athenaeus extracts a list of figs: Androtion, Philip, and Hegemon (3.75d). The satirical drama *Agen* is attributed to two authors, Python, about whom it is not known whether he was from Catania or from Byzantium, and Alexander the Great himself (2.50f; the bibliographic "index card" is repeated at 13.586d). The habit of sacrificing pigs to Aphrodite is documented through an historical work from which Athenaeus quotes one sentence. But is that work by Callimachus or by Zenodotus (3.95f–96a)? In some cases, Athenaeus takes a position in favor of a given attribution, but also mentions the other one, perhaps for the benefit of his bibliophile readers who could be driven to look for the book in a library or in the shop of a bookseller: "As Chameleon of Pontus says in his treatise *On Pleasure* (which however is also attributed to Theophrastus)" (6.273c). Or else, even while attributing the text to an author, Athenaeus suggests that that attribution is debatable: "Pherecrates, or whoever wrote the *Cheiron*" (9.388f); "Polemon, or whoever the author of the text entitled *The Book of Greece* was" (11.479f). The problem was traditionally raised by ancient poetic texts. When he cites the *Cypria*, Athenaeus mentions, not without a certain carelessness, the traditional problem of the identification of their author: "whether it is a Cypriot, or Stasinus, or whether he bears the names he likes most" (8.334b–c), or whether it is Hegesias, Stasinus, or Cyprias of Halicarnassus (15.682d–e).

A close and exhaustive examination of all those bibliographical anomalies would make it possible to trace an evocative picture of the state of textual transmission at the time of Athenaeus, and of the doubts and discussions that had arisen regarding it.[29] Every literary genre raised specific problems. Comedies, abundantly cited, often had a double attribution, perhaps the result of homonymy that at some point had caused confusion. Thus a quotation from the *Skeuai*,[30] mediated by Chameleon, is attributed to Aristophanes and to Plato (14.628e; see also 14.642d). The tradition of Hippocratic treatises also raises specific problems: Athenaeus thus mentions alternative titles under which the treatise *On Diet* circulated: *On Acute Diseases, On Barley-gruel*, or *A Response to the Cnidian Maxims* (2.45e–f).

Every book collector also had to take on the question of homonymous authors, a factor creating considerable confusion. Diogenes Laertius even made it the concluding remark of some of his *Lives of the Philosophers*.[31] This explains the care taken by Athenaeus in specifying the identity of the authors he cites through a geographic qualification, reference to a literary genre, or an established intellectual discipline. This does not prevent him from citing side by side in the same sentence Plato the philosopher and Plato the comic (for example 2.48a; 7.314a). In some cases, however, the ambiguity cannot be resolved: when Plato the comic alludes to Philoxenus' *Banquet*, is it Philoxenus of Cythera or Philoxenus of Leucas (4.146f)? However, the bibliophiles had at their disposal specialized aids that allowed them to avoid the traps into which ignorant collectors must have invariably fallen. One such aid is the treatise *On Homonymous Poets and Writers* by Demetrius of Magnesia (13.611b), a first-century BC scholar and a friend of Atticus, cited by Cicero, criticized by Dionysius of Halicarnassus, and abundantly quoted by Diogenes Laertius.[32] And a similar work by Heraclides of Mopsus allows Athenaeus to obtain the list of all the authors named Polemon (6.234c–d). Ulpian, as we have seen, consults his companions on Chrysippus and Harpocration, asking them in which library have they found those homonyms of famous authors (14.648c).

---

29   On this question one can refer to multiple contributions in Braund and Wilkins 2000, especially those by E. Bowie on elegiac and iambic poetry, by K. Sidwell on fifth-century comedy, by G. Zecchini on Athenaeus and Harpocration, by F. Walbank on Polybius, and by C. Pelling on the use of the historians. See also Zecchini 1989.

30   The meaning of this title is unclear. "Costumes" (Kaibel)? "Goods and Chattels" (Gulick)?

31   See e.g. 2.103–4 (Theodore); 5.83–85 (Demetrius); 5.93–94 (Heraclides); 6.81 (Diogenes); 9.17 (Heraclitus); 9.49 (Democritus).

32   Cicero, *Letters to Atticus* 4.11.1–2; 8.11.7; 8.12.6; 9.9.2; Dionysius of Halicarnassus, *On Dinarchus* 1; Diogenes Laertius, *Lives of the Eminent Philosophers* 1.38, 79, 112, 114; 2.52, 56, 57; 5.3, 75, 89; 6.79, 84, 88; 7.31, 169, 185; 8.85; 9.15, 27, 35–36, 40; 10.13. It is significant that Diogenes Laertius does not include Demetrius of Magnesia in his list of homonymous authors called "Demetrius" (5.83–85). Demetrius of Magnesia was also the author of a treatise *On Homonymous Cities*. See *RE* 4.2.2814–17 (Schwartz); *FHG* 4.382.

Larensis' guests could have doubts on the authenticity of some texts, doubts that were inspired by the philological criticism of the great centers of knowledge in the Hellenistic world. They also show their mastery of that philological tradition when they mention the critical judgments of the grammarians, nevertheless justifying their choice to quote a suspect text: for example, Hesiod's *Marriage of Ceyx*, "since, even though the grammarians have withdrawn from the poet the paternity of that work, it nevertheless seems to me to be ancient" (2.49b). They can also contest the authenticity of a passage, for example those verses in Hesiod, reported by Euthydemus of Athens in his book *On Salted Fish*, which are more reminiscent of the style of a cook than of the more musical of poets, and which allude to places that Hesiod could not have known: Parion, Byzantium, Tarentum, and Campania. For the grammarian Leonidas, those verses are in all probability by Euthydemus himself. "Whose the verses are, dearest Leonidas, it is up to you most excellent grammarians, to decide. But since now the conversation shifts to salted fish...," answers Dionysocles (3.116a–d).

More recent authors do not escape such investigation: Athenaeus cites Theophrastus' *Monarchy*, dedicated to Cassander, adding an aside: "If this treatise is authentic, since many hold that it is by Sosibius" (4.144e). The corpus of Attic orators also poses problems, and Athenaeus voices the doubts of the learned tradition on the authenticity of such-and-such a speech by Lysias (6.231b: *On the Golden Tripod*; 13.586e and 592e: *Against Lais*; see also 13.586e–f and 592c: *Against Philonides*), by Hyperides (13.566f: *Against Patroclus*) or by Demosthenes (13.573b and 586e: *Against Neaera*).[33] The suspicion is expressed, but does not discourage the quotation.

Everything indicates that Athenaeus and his characters mastered the great works of reference of ancient bibliography. Democritus testifies in a noteworthy way to this recourse to bibliographic finding aids in a library of imperial times when he tries to verify the existence of a comedy by Alexis, *The Master of Debaucheries*, cited by the Peripatetic Sotion of Alexandria (8.336d).[34] Now, Democritus had never come across that comedy, despite the breadth of his reading (according to his own account, he had read more than eight hundred plays of Middle Comedy), and neither did he find mention of it in Callimachus' *Pinakes*, nor in the supplement and the corrections by Aristophanes of Byzantium, nor in the catalogues of the librarians of Pergamon. It was therefore an unobtainable book, whose existence, however, Democritus never doubts: in a way he is even proud to have found mention of this comedy, which had escaped

---

[33] Athenaeus thus testifies to the critical debates on the constitution of the corpus of the Attic orators, where Dionysius of Halicarnassus and Caecilius of Calacte pursued the work of Callimachus. See Dover 1968:15–22.

[34] See Arnott 1996:819–22.

the best Hellenistic bibliographers. Their catalogues were thus still required reading for a second-century scholar who had much on his hands given all the identification problems related to a specific book.[35]

Athenaeus testifies to the use of the hundred and twenty rolls of Callimachus' *Tables of Those who Distinguished Themselves in the Fields of Culture, and of the Works Written by Them*. The work was more than a catalogue: it was a systematic bibliography of literary genres and fields of knowledge, with all the information necessary to identify books and situate their authors. Perhaps through indirect sources, Athenaeus thus refers to the sections devoted to the "various treatises" (6.244a; 14.643e–f), to the speeches (15.669d–e), and to the laws (13.585b). In Callimachus he finds bibliographies: for example, a list of works on pastry (14.643e–f), or on authors of *Banquets*, which opened by mentioning Chaerephon, accompanied by the beginning of the text and by the number of verses (6.244a; see also 13.585b, on Gnathaena).[36] Other bibliographies appear in Athenaeus: for example, one on the authors of treatises on fishing, in prose or in verse (1.13b), on tragic dance (1.20d), on cookery books (12.516c), on the comedies bearing the names of famous courtesans (13.567c–d).

Callimachus also offers information that can be biographical, like the name of Lysimachus' philosophy master (6.252c), or bibliographical, like an alternative title for a comedy by Diphylus (11.496e–f). Aristophanes of Byzantium, who had revised Callimachus' *Pinakes*, is also cited in relation to questions of lexicography, which shows how the librarian-like treatment of books allowed one to deal with the form and substance of the texts (9.408f; 410b–c). Athenaeus knows of the existence of other manuals, such as *Collections of Books*, by Artemon of Cassandrea (12.515d–e). By the same author, Athenaeus also cites *On the Usefulness of Books*, although the title of this work might simply refer to a section of the previous one (15.694a). This author should perhaps be identified with Artemon of Pergamon (around 100 BC), mentioned in the *scholia* to Pindar.[37] Artemon was in any case representative of Pergamene bibliographic science, and Athenaeus cites him in order to contest, based on an argument of chronological impossibility, his attribution of a historical treatise to Dionysius Skytobrachion. Athenaeus also cites him for his typology of *skolia*: indeed, Artemon's second book was devoted to the various sorts of convivial songs. That manual may have integrated bibliography and literary history, designed as it was to serve the bibliophiles who wished to put together their own library. Tradition has preserved the titles of other

---

[35] See also Dionysius of Halicarnassus, *On Dinarchus* 1.

[36] There is no other mention of this Chaerephon in the *Deipnosophists*. Callimachus' entry is one testimony among others concerning that famous parasite.

[37] See *FHG* 4.342, *FGrHist* 32.T.6, and *Kommentar* 510; *RE* 2.2.1446ff. (Wentzel); R. Goulet, s.v. "Artemon", in *DphA* 1.434, p. 615ff.

similar works, not cited by Athenaeus: *On the Acquisition and Selection of Books*, by Herennius Philo (a contemporary of Hadrian), and *On the Knowledge of Books*, by Telephus of Pergamon, where the author noted the books that were worth acquiring.[38]

---

[38]   The very rare *testimonia* are collected in *RE* 15.653ff (Gudeman) and *RE* 19.369–79 (Wendel).

13

Scholars' Practices

THE BIBLIOGRAPHICAL KNOWLEDGE of Athenaeus and his characters is of a cartographical nature; it organizes a space, subdivides it, and proposes different points of view, which lead from the literary genre to the text and to the quotation, or vice versa. This shift in the hierarchy between container and contained corresponds to a change of scale and to specific forms of articulation: the articulation of sections of the library, literary genres, works within the corpus of an author, books, the rolls that compose them, and the words that fill them.

Callimachus' *Pinakes* are, in practice, the map of a library aimed to cover the totality of *paideia*. That orientation-table traces the horizon shared by the deipnosophists, even if, after Callimachus, the strata of erudition, Hellenistic first, then imperial, were deposited on the Alexandrian base, to which they brought the additional depth of learned monographs, philological conjectures, lexica, and commentaries. However, the structure of the map itself was not subject to change, since it was based on the inventory and the ordering of the literary and intellectual heritage of classical Greece. Even though the map was enriched by inevitable corrections and additions of detail, it was not modified by them. Rather, it acquired relief, thanks to the development of a metaliterature which is a center of activity, in commentary, edition, collection of words, facts, and quotations, all according to the creation of new objects of knowledge. The *Deipnosophists* are but a stage in a history which is still ongoing today.

The members of Larensius' circle master a certain number of literary techniques which allow them to situate themselves on that map in its two dimensions, horizontal and vertical. They have at their disposal an intellectual arsenal to take advantage of that library and "work" the quotations they extract from it, with the aim of producing collectively, in the course of their convivial conversations, a form of knowledge. Those literary practices take the form of a group of gestures, that range from the most concrete (handling books) to the most abstract (interpreting, criticizing, commenting, correlating). The literary form chosen by Athenaeus, a polyphony of speeches that follow the development of the table conversations, stresses the construction of knowledge, and not only its objective content. Unlike a lexicon or an encyclopedia, which, if anything, use objective information without clarifying its origin, Athenaeus privileges a reflexive and dialectical dimension within which his characters make explicit their praxis, their intellectual tools, and their criteria of judgment. The *Deipnosophists* thus offers a privileged testimony on the expertise of scholars, and introduces us into the heart of the practices of a circle of grammarians, rhetoricians, physicians, and musicians who share, beyond their different specialties, the same basic techniques.

To present those techniques would involve taking into account all the components of imperial literary culture. Knowledge distinguished ordinary reading from specialized reading, capable of resolving the difficulties that one comes against in reading ancient texts. That knowledge is mentioned in general terms, as an indispensible prerequisite to understanding, for example, an epigram by Simonides (10.456e). However, it also manifests itself in the course of the text, both within the conversations of the deipnosophists and within the *Deipnosophists* which relates them, since Athenaeus remains the director of all those literary games. This grammatical culture manifests itself, for example, in the procedures necessary to solve a problem of interpretation relating to a word used by Anacreon: to collect the corpus of previously suggested solutions, discuss them, and look for complementary information in specialized treatises (14.634b–636c). It also comes through in the isolated explanations brought to a text in the very course of its recitation, the oral equivalent of the "marginal notes" or "footnotes" around a written text: the comment, "by 'leaves' he means not those of the fig tree, but those of the poppy," is specified in a parenthesis during the quotation of the list of flowers used for crowns contained in Nicander's *Georgica* (15.684a). These scholars are conscious of the necessity of verifying the texts they read, comparing several copies if necessary, and noting their significant variants: this is what happens with the work of Nicander himself (15.684c). The deipnosophists do not hesitate to discuss the conjectures of the Alexandrine editors, conscious of the importance of the establishment of the text for the interpretation of the meaning of the works that they read. It could simply be a question of modifying the punctuation of a verse of Homer (1.12 a–b), of comparing three verses of Eubulus with Alexis (1.25f–26a), of endorsing Aristarchus' suggestion concerning the suppression of a verse of the *Iliad* (2.39d), or of noting the different orthography of a word in Hesiod and in various copies of Antiphanes' *Minos* (2.58d).[1]

---

[1]   Other references of philological interest: 2.61c; 3.85e–f; 5.177c, 178d, 180c–d, 180e–181a, 188f, 193a–b; 7.323f–324a, 329d; 9.397c; 11.492a, 493a, 498f; 13.592d; 14.634c–d, 649c–d.

I shall dwell at greater length on three fundamental operations: reading *per se*, memorization, and techniques of investigation.

Indeed, before anything else, our characters are great readers: "considering that you have often spoken of meat, poultry, and pigeon, I am also ready to tell you what I have been able to discover regarding these by virtue of my very wide-ranging reading (*poluanagnōsia*), without repeating what has already been said," says one of the interlocutors when the "second tables" are at the center of the conversation (14.654a). The guests sometimes reproach each other for their lack of judgment in their reading choices. Cynulcus, for example: "You are devoid of culture, my dear table companions, because you do not read the only books that could educate those who desire the beautiful; I mean the *Silloi* by Timon, the disciple of Pyrrhon" (4.159e–160a), but in this case it is the taunt of a Cynic.

Reading has an exploratory and heuristic function: it provides Athenaeus' characters with the material for their conversations, where the rules seem to be, like in Callimachus' learned poetry, that nothing should be said that is not based on the evidence of a source.[2] Reading is thus collecting interesting facts, words, and quotations—in sum, everything that is worth mentioning and remembering at the same time. Although the deipnosophists share the same library, they are nevertheless very different with respect to what they can gather from it and with respect to what attracts their interest as they are reading. "While reading the twenty-eighth book of Poseidonius' *Histories*, I found, my friends, an absolutely delicious passage on perfumes, a passage that would not be out of place in our *sumposion*" (15.692c). The talent of that reader lies in offering a paradoxical point of view on the work of Poseidonius, taking the Stoic to task on a question of minor importance if to the point, while his treatise without doubt included more serious content. Reading means taking note and memorizing, so as to reactivate the memory of a read passage during a conversation, or, possibly, in the writing of a new text. Thus, one may have read Phylarchus' entire *History*, as in the case of Myrtilus, without having noted the passage of Book 23 on the cities of Ceos, where there are neither prostitutes nor flute-players; a passage that on the contrary, did not escape Cynulcus (13.610d).

Democritus corresponds well to the profile of a great reader when he declares that he has read over eight hundred plays of Middle Comedy, and that he gathered extracts from them (8.336d). In this case reading is accompanied by writing, used to copy the chosen passages. The principles on which that selection was made, as well as the concrete procedure of transcription, are not defined: is the material put together by play? Or redistributed by keyword, in alphabetical order, by theme? The extracts, in any case, show the course taken

---

[2]   Callimachus, fr. 612 Pfeiffer.

by a systematic reader who aspired to a certain degree of exhaustiveness, at least within a specific literary genre; they also reveal his taste, his intellectual interests, and what he wishes to accumulate and put in his treasury in order to be able to consult it later at his leisure.

From that point of view, Ulpian is often the target of his companions' teasing. Cynulcus, in particular, distances himself from his reading procedures: "In fact, when I read, I do not extract the thorns from the book, like you do, but what is most useful and worth hearing" (15.671c). Already in Book 8 Cynulcus had criticized Ulpian for not choosing anything but the bones of the smallest fish, neglecting the slices of large fish (8.347d–e). Ulpian in turn expressed his objections to Cynulcus' manner of reading, "since you are the one who, in books, not only chooses but unearths the most hidden things" (15.678f).

The characters of Athenaeus thus devote themselves to an activity characteristic of the scholars of Hellenistic and imperial times: they take reading notes so as to collect and order raw material destined to be reused in new erudite writings or during conversations.[3] Besides, the banquet conversation lent itself particularly well to that sort of exhibition and one could prepare a repertoire of quotations and lines precisely in view of such meetings. Thus, at the beginning of his work, in a section that is unfortunately epitomized, Athenaeus mentions the figure of Charmus of Syracuse who had verses and proverbs ready for each course of the banquet. As for Calliphanes, he prepared by copying the three or four first verses of a certain number of poems (1.4a–c). Next to those practices of dilettanti who wished to give themselves a patina of erudition, the

---

[3] The question was recently taken up and discussed by Dorandi 2000, Chapter 2, "Legere, adnotare, excerpere." The testimony of Pliny the Younger on his uncle's working methods (*Letters* 3.5) shows a complex organization where the scholar was aided by slaves who acted as research assistants. Pliny could thus fill the books he read with reference marks that would indicate to the slaves the passages to be copied. He could also dictate the extracts he wanted to keep directly to a slave, who then noted them on a tablet. Those extracts were then redistributed in the rolls of *commentarii*, presumably classified by subject. One may wonder if the fact that those rolls were inscribed on both sides (*opisthographi*) cannot be explained by the necessity to insert in the thematic sections that were quickly filled the constant flow of new quotations without having to copy the totality of the roll in order to find the right place for them. The quotations and notes collected from the original texts could thus pass through several stages of transcription: first tablets, then classified rolls of documentation, before being reused in the final text. The context described by Pliny can without doubt explain the genesis of the *Deipnosophists*, and makes it possible for us to imagine Athenaeus receiving the help of Larensius' slaves in order to collect and classify his immense documentation. To this work of recomposition of compiled material one can oppose the method of Aulus Gellius, who at the beginning of his *Attic Nights* declares he has followed the haphazard order of his reading notes. See also Photius, *Bibliotheca* 175.119b.27–32, concerning Pamphile, a woman of letters who had put into writing thirteen years of reading notes and materials taken during her conversations. On the quotation and compilation methods of ancient authors see also Helmbold and O'Neil 1959; Skydsgaard 1968; van den Hoek 1996.

deipnosophists appear in the guise of authentic scholars who have read their texts from beginning to end, or at least who boast they did, and have compiled them in a comprehensive enough manner to be able to use the words and quotations suitable for the various moments of the conversation.

Athenaeus, however, does not present his characters as busy unrolling without pause their rolls of reading notes. Most of the time, the deipnosophists quote from memory. The books that fill their bags only seem to be used for the reading of long extracts, like those from the *Dinner-Party Letters* of Lynceus and Hippolochus, or the treatise by Callixeinus of Rhodes. Books were used to make up for memory's failings. In the list of fish, for example, Athenaeus mentions the effects of the torpedo (*narkē*); the person speaking states: "Clearchus of Soli offered an explanation of this in his book *On the Torpedo*, but I have forgotten that long passage and refer you to the treatise" (7.314c). Quotation is intimately linked to the exercise of memory. The deipnosophists thus run through their mental libraries, where the memories of their readings are stored.

The practice of speaking on imposed subjects during the conversation is designed to mobilize those memories, and in a way to read what is written in the wax tablets of memory: "I shall say what occurs to me (*ta moi prospiptonta*)," says Magnus as he opens his speech on figs (3.74c–d). And that is precisely the exercise to which our characters devote themselves: to quote impromptu and on the spot (4.175e), to search (*anapempazesthai*) in what had been read long ago (6.263a–b), and to search within their memory for occurrences of a rare word which they know had been used by ancient authors (8.362a).

When one has to recite sequences of quotations, it is essential to master the ordering principle that allows one to co-ordinate them, the *taxis*. An example might be the chronological succession of poets or of theatrical performances (it is Democritus, the specialist of New Comedy, who uses this principle: 6.268d–e); or else, the alphabetical order, chosen by Athenaeus to organize his list of names of fish, in such a way that Timocrates could memorize it with ease (7.277c); or great subdivisions, like the ones that structure the impressive list devoted to *truphē* in Book 12, where examples ordered according to ethnographic criteria are followed by the enumeration of individual cases. Even the food, with the *taxis* of the dishes served in turn, offer both the deipnosophists and Athenaeus himself a convenient thread that gives an order to the quotations (15.665b); and when he is about to begin his "erotic list", Athenaeus calls on the muse Erato to support his memory (13.555a–b).

Yet there are several degrees of memory. One can remember a source without being capable of quoting it literally (3.127c), or cite it thinking one possesses it to the letter (8.332b–c). One can be incapable of telling a story from memory when the book was read too long ago (8.359d–e); or, in spite of that, one can remember the "voice" (*phōnē*) of the author and cite it (11.461a). One can quote literally for a particular interest or a personal motive: "I know his words backwards because they are very dear to me," says Cynulcus quoting Clearchus on the Phagesia (7.275d). It sometimes happens that one has a memory blank, and apologies are given for the incident, as occurs for example when the list of sacrificial flat breads and sweets contained in a work of Aristomenes of Athens is about to be recited (3.115a). In such cases, the reader at least is referred to a bibliographical source.

When the memory of a guest fails, it is another who cites the text (for instance at 3.107b). We are in a space of shared memory which is under everyone's control. It is a question of reviving a common knowledge: "You all know, I suppose, what our noble Herodotus said on Panionius of Chios" (6.266e). When Ulpian gives up using the word *mustros* "because it cannot be found in any of our predecessors," Aemilianus criticises him: "You are losing your memory, my admirable Ulpian: have you not always admired Nicander of Colophon, the epic poet, for his love of the ancients and for his erudition?" (3.126b).

Being capable of quoting texts from memory is a characteristic of the educated man (*pepaideumenos*), even if he is a slave (3.108d: Myrtilus' slave) or a cook (3.102b; 9.381f–382a). Indeed, learning poetry or extracts of theatrical plays by heart was a common school exercise, and reciting those texts was among the pastimes of cultivated Greeks (4.164a; 8.335e; 11.482d; 12.537d; 14.620b; 15.693f–694a). However, the deipnosophists were not satisfied only with quoting texts learnt by heart. They had special techniques that allowed them to navigate within the corpus of memorized texts. Indeed, being able to find the verse, phrase, or word required by a particular moment in the conversation presupposes the capacity to move in a non-linear manner either among texts learned by heart or in collections of fragments and quotations that were previously isolated: while the recitation of a poem follows the order of the verses from beginning to end, Athenaeus' characters are capable of immediately recalling to memory a particular verse, and of putting it in relation with a verse of another composition. That non-linear memory suggests a form of mental indexing that makes it possible to produce series of quotations ordered according to the same keyword. Mnemotechnics make up for the limits of the ancient book, the papyrus roll, where the columns of text succeeded each other linearly without pagination or numbering of the lines of text, without an *index nominum* or an *index verborum*. Finding a specific passage in a roll was not impossible: a sign put in the margin of the column could serve as a point of reference, as can be seen from the practice of the Alexandrian philologists, who equipped the margins of the text's columns with diacritical signs. When, however, it was a matter of mobilizing scores of quotations on a single theme or a keyword, as Athenaeus' characters are doing, looking for occurrences directly in books turned out to be an absolutely impossible operation. Without doubt, the lexica and glossaries had the function of providing a great number of quotations, and specialized treatises on the most disparate subjects also collected material extracted from the literary sources. The rolls of reading notes, where the scholars organized their extracts, supplied an instrument of personal archiving; Athenaeus and his characters make great use of it. However, in their conversations, the deipnosophists consult neither lexica nor reading notes, but resort to their memory. Is that a literary fiction that hides the work of compilation done by Athenaeus? Perhaps. Yet the practice of quotation represented in those terms also corresponds to an effective form of "gymnastics of the mind,"[4] which consists in moving within memorized texts as one would move within a concrete book-roll, whose reading could be interrupted and resumed at any line of the text.[5]

A quotation from Clearchus in Book 10, mentions the pastimes practiced during the banquets of the ancients. A guest, for example, began by quoting an epic or iambic verse, and his neighbor had to quote the following one. Someone else would quote a passage, and then one had to quote another author who illustrated the same idea. Or, everyone had to recite an iambic verse. It was possible to add specific rules, like the obligation to quote a verse composed of a certain number of syllables. One also enjoyed reciting the names of the chiefs of the Achaeans or the Trojans, or the names of cities in Asia that began with a given letter; the neighbor then cited a city in Europe, Greek or barbarian. For Clearchus that game raised everyone's learning (10.457e–f). Memory of texts, names, things: from the literary quotation to the recitation of Homeric catalogue, those games presupposed a well-trained memory, and the mastery of a corpus of epic and iambic texts within which one was capable of moving freely.

To illustrate those pastimes, and in that way to test his mnemotechnical virtuosity, the narrator (perhaps still Aemilianus: 10.448b) provides a certain number of examples: quoting verses from Homer that begin and end with alpha; then, iambic verses. Next, the same operation with the letter epsilon, then with eta, iota, sigma, and omega. One could then enjoy citing verses without a sigma, or verses from Homer in which the first and last syllables each form a name, or even verses in which the first and last syllables, when put together, formed a word with a complete meaning describing an object or a foodstuff (10.458a–f).

---

[4] See Cribiore 2001.

[5] The ancient sources on the art of memory (essentially the *Rhetorica ad Herennium* and Quintilian's *Institutio Oratoria*) give primary importance to its application to rhetoric: it is at the same time a principle of composition of the speech and an aid for oratory performance. There were certainly other applications of that technique, in particular for scholars and grammarians. For a presentation of the questions, see Small 1997.

Exercises of this sort put aural memory into play, and again, the capacity to choose and combine in a non-linear way texts that had been learned by heart, isolating verse, word, and syllable. Was every educated Greek who knew his *Iliad* and his iambic poetry by heart also capable of such gymnastics of the mind? Does a digression such as that by Aemilianus not also have the function of offering the reader some examples ready to be reused without much effort in a traditional party game?

The deipnosophists extend this game to the entire library. Their challenges and their exchanges consist in putting together when they speak the highest number of quotations extracted from various texts. If, as in the case of King Cassander mentioned by Athenaeus (14.620b), a cultured Greek, educated at the school of the grammarians, could know by heart large extracts of the Homeric poems (when he did not know them integrally),[6] it is difficult to believe that the deipnosophists had memorized in their entirety the works they cite. The meaning of the word "memorization", however, needs to be clarified: to quote a passage literally is not the same as to paraphrase its content, or to know that this piece of information can be found "somewhere" in a given book. Thus a vague assertion based on an inaccurate memory ("Hegesander spoke of the citrus somewhere, but I don't remember where.") does not resist the certainties of someone who has just finished reading the entire text and certifies that, in that text, there is no mention of citrus whatsoever (3.83a–c). That notwithstanding, the fact remains that the quotations rely on memorized texts, and that the listeners are able to control and verify the quotations of others by confronting them with their memory of the texts. Inviting Ulpian to start his catalogue of flower crowns, Myrtilus takes care to ask him not to cite the treatise *On Crowns* by Aelius Asclepiades, because it is known to everyone (15.676e–f).

Myrtilus (as we have seen) says he has read the entire *History* of Phylarchus and does not remember a passage to which Cynulcus is alluding (13.610d). Why does Cynulcus remember that passage? Perhaps because like Democritus and Ulpian he practices the exercise of *eklogē*, the selection and extraction of noteworthy passages from the text he has read. Cynulcus is thus an indefatigable examiner who digs through books in search of their secrets (15.678f). The extracts collected from those readings had the function of selecting and choosing materials, and of making them easy to memorize, in this case, by redistributing them in papyrus rolls according to thematic criteria. Besides, Athenaeus' *Deipnosophists* can also be considered as an ample collection of those reading notes, ready to be learned by heart by readers eager to transform a

---

[6] See e.g. Plato, *Protagoras* 325a; Xenophon, *Symposium* 3.6.

Roman *cena* into an Attic *sumposion*, or to have at their disposal in reduced form (fifteen books) a condensed library.

Athenaeus' particularity resides in presenting that process of recollection and that itinerary within the library in the form of a collective oral performance, in the mutual exchange and polyphony of a conversation. The mnemotechnical virtuosity of the deipnosophists is at the level of their excellence in the field of *paideia*. It is difficult to escape the temptation to associate their performances with what Eunapius tells us of the sophist Longinus, one of Porphyry's masters: Longinus was a sort of "living library" (*bibliothēkē tis ... empsuchos*) and a "wandering museum" (*peripatoun mouseion*).[7] Under the guidance of Longinus, Porphyry indeed reached the culminating point of *paideia*, at the summit of grammar and rhetoric. The author of many works, Longinus distinguished himself especially by his critique of the ancients, and in literary circles his judgment reigned supreme among his contemporaries.

Why this strange status for Longinus? A library and a museum at the same time, he is, so to speak, an entire Alexandria by himself. He embodies Alexandria's erudition and critical authority, and his works fill the libraries of others. He also, however, bases his judgments on his knowledge of the works of the ancients, and that living library is in effect an incorporated, memorized library. Eunapius' description could easily be applied to Athenaeus' characters: to Ulpian, Masurius, Larensius (whose profound critical sense is highlighted from the very beginning of the work: 1.2b), or to Charmadas, that Greek mentioned by Pliny the Elder who, when shown a book in a library, was able to recite it by heart as if he were reading it.[8] The specific techniques that could allow one to forge a memory of that sort are attested by Seneca, who mentions his contemporary Calvisius Sabinus, who had bought at high price slaves trained to be living books: each one had learned one classical author by heart—Homer, Hesiod, or the Lyrics—and had the suitable quotations ready at the disposal of their forgetful master during the banquet conversations.[9] The wealth of Sabinus' library depended on the number of living books that he had succeeded in putting together: some Greek classics, it would seem, were sufficient. Unfortunately, Sabinus also had a very weak short-term memory, and he was unable to repeat the quotations his living books whispered to his ears.

Reading in one's memory as if one held a book. Pliny's Charmadas could illustrate one of the rules of ancient mnemotechnics: things are written in

---

[7] Eunapius, *Lives of the Sophists* 455ff. On this text see Too 2000:111–23 and Too 2010.

[8] Pliny, *Natural History* 7.24. On the library as a model for structuring memory, see also Vitruvius, *On Architecture* 7.praef. 4.

[9] Seneca, *Moral Letters to Lucilius* 3.27.5, a passage that can be compared to Larensius' criticism of the Romans who make their cooks learn the dialogues of Plato (9.381f–382a).

memory as they are written on tablets or papyrus rolls. To remember is to read.[10] Material books and libraries are the model of the immaterial books and libraries of memory.[11]

Keeping in mind the deipnosophists' words so as to report them to Timocrates, Athenaeus reproduces on a macro-structural level the performance of his own characters (7.277b; 14.643d; 15.665a–b). Like them, he has to search his memory (*anapempazesthai*), not for what he read but for what they said (10.459b–c). However, contrary to his characters, most of the time he remembers entire, continuous speeches, and has less frequent recourse to that form of combinatorial and non-linear memory we have analyzed.[12] In the narrative frame of the *Deipnosophists*, Athenaeus reconstructs from memory the long thread of the banquet's conversation, the succession of speakers, and all the texts and authors each of them quoted. This recollection process is duplicated: first, in the oral account of Athenaeus to Timocrates, and second, in the transcription of this account in fifteen book-rolls. Athenaeus was too erudite to ignore the tradition about the invention of the art of memory. The poet Simonides of Cos was able to identify the corpses of Scopas and his guests, after the roof of the banquet room fell and crushed them all, since he remembered the position of each of them on the couches around the table.[13] This is the founding myth of ancient mnemotechnics, relying on a system of organized places where one can store information, either facts and ideas or literal quotations. In order to retrieve this content, one has to go through these mental places and to activate the data stored in each of them. Athenaeus relies on two different systems of mnemonic places: the first one is the organization of the banquet room, where the guests are lying on couches around central tables; the second one is the sequence of events and dishes, from the very beginning of the banquet to the end of the symposium. The mix of these two systems allows Athenaeus to reconstruct the entire thread of the conversation, linking together the speakers and the topics they discussed.

In the *Deipnosophists* memory is performance, and as such it is inseparable from the interaction of the guests. What sets it in motion is the game of questions and challenges that takes place within Larensius' circle; what sets off recollection is the *zētēsis*, a technique of investigation and framing of questions that invites one to explore the libraries of the mind. *Zētēsis* is inseparable from a mode of experiencing culture and knowledge: this is attested by Ulpian,

---

[10]   *Rhetorica ad Herennium* 3.19.32.
[11]   On the fate of this model in the Middle Ages, see Carruthers 1990.
[12]   See however 7.277b–c and 14.616e, where Athenaeus reconfigures the materials of the deipnosophists according to ordering criteria different from the ones they spell out.
[13]   Cicero, *On the Orator* 2.86; Quintilian, *Institutio Oratoria* 11.2.11–22.

the investigator *par excellence*, symposiarch and promoter of the game of the dialogue (1.1d–e). *Zētēsis* is, in its proper sense, "the search for solutions, explanations or responses to a given question": this intellectual activity can mobilize the most profound critical capacities, and Larensius' eulogy mentions his skill in that art (1.2b–3b). Finding the answer requires secure erudition, and sometimes time, many interlocutors, and the luck of coming across a book that gives the solution (15.676e–f). It is also a social activity, which presupposes a search for interlocutors, an audience, the pleasure of searching together, and of being the first to find the goal. The banquet, the place and time of distraction and *paideia*, provides a privileged framework for this party game,[14] but Ulpian (as we have seen) also practiced it in the streets, the baths, and the shops of booksellers. So is it a matter of finding the correct answer to the questions? Or of finding answers whatever the cost? The deipnosophists provide answers that complete each other, that add nuances, and sometimes that contradict each other. The *zētēsis* is the driving force behind the conversation and the exchanges and it modulates the rhythm of the interventions, facilitating some to suggest solutions while others search in silence (3.83a–c). That way of proceeding is strongly criticized by Cynulcus (3.97c), but in fact he is himself a virtuoso of it (3.106e), although in less obsessive a manner than Ulpian.

Zētēsis is an essential operator in Athenaeus' text: it allows the passage from things to words, from food to discourse on food, from table to library, from one guest to the other one. The passing of dishes and the ritualized unfolding of the meeting automatically impose the subjects of research, so that the deipnosophists do not need to use their imagination or to negotiate the appropriate themes like the guests of Plutarch.[15] Formulating a question, however, stimulates constant and reflexive attention to what is being said, done and seen in the course of the meeting.

A *zētēsis* is a trigger that sets in motion the process of recollection, that combinatorial selection within the mental library that precedes sequences of quotations. Proposing a simple question (who? why? where? what is it?), it offers a thread that allows one to trace a path through the labyrinth of words. Of course, the *zētēsis* concerning the feet or ears of pigs, or even liver sausages (3.107a–b), may seem to be of restricted interest, except from the point of view of cooking and nutrition, but the point is probably not there: the *zētēsis* is an exercise of mental gymnastics, necessary for the maintenance, activation, and enrichment of the library of memorized texts that every guest carries within him, and also

---

[14]   See 5.188d–e: *zētēsis* was already present in Menelaus' banquet in the *Odyssey*; 10.420c: during the banquets of the philosopher Menedemus the guests devoted themselves to *zētēseis* (satirical drama by Lycophron). See also 13.585e.

[15]   The books read by them also generated their store of questions: e.g. 15.669d, 670f, 671d–672a.

necessary to that feeling of mastery (*kratein*) of a linguistic configuration and a cultural universe that now belong in the past, preserved in writing, but possible to reactivate through orality. *Zētēsis* creates a contest between the guests as to who will be the quickest to answer. There should be no latency period between the moment when the *zētēsis* is issued and when the series of answers starts coming (3.119b, 125d). Sometimes Ulpian gives the answer before asking the question (3.125a); at other times, the companions anticipate his question and immediately give the answer (5.209e-f). They all make it a point of honor not to leave Ulpian's questions unanswered, even at the cost of sharing the achievement (6.234c-d).

Asking questions about whatever exists in the world, seizing on words and attributing a problematic strangeness to them: that is the sport to which Ulpian devotes himself, often knitting his brows (9.385b); that way he fills an essential function in Athenaeus' text, since he is the one who initiates changes of subject in the conversation, both in the progressive specification of the topics and through explicit digressions (3.115b). Others less gifted than he could find in books lists of problems ready to be used in the conversation, together with their solutions: the written text thus came to compensate for blanks in the memory and erudition of his readers.[16]

This intellectual exercise appears in the form of a real party game that is not devoid of didactic implications, a game to which the members of Larensius' circle devote themselves with pleasure, with a sense of humor yet at times grudgingly: "We feed on questions," remembers the house master himself (9.398b). This collective procedure for the production of knowledge clearly perpetuates techniques that were in use in the Athenian philosophical schools and in the Museum of Alexandria itself.[17] Athenaeus privileges a model of inquiry that requires simple and immediate answers, but does not ignore the fact that *zētēsis* could also take on more complex questions, real riddles on which generations of scholars had practiced their skills, and *zētēsis* had given rise to a specialized literature that expounded the problems and sometimes the solutions as well (see e.g. 3.85e; 15.673d–674b). Those banquets devoted to all sorts of philological, literary, and lexical research suggest a further analogy between Larensius' circle and the Museum of Alexandria. According to Porphyry, the Museum's

---

[16] See 7.276a: Clearchus provides a large number of *problēmata*. Plutarch's *Symposiacs* sometimes lose sight of the setting of the symposium in order to present problems of the competence of the physical and natural sciences in the Aristotelian tradition. The desire of scholars to master the solution of famous problems could lead them to theft or plagiarism: see 15.673d–674b, the episode of Anacreon's "rush crowns". On the *zētēsis* of the very erudite Aristotle see 15.692b, with a quotation from the *Problemata Physika*.

[17] See the observations made by Romeri on the verbs *proballō* and *proteinō*, and the Aristotelian use of *problēma* and *protasis* in Romeri 2000:564n13.

scholars were in the habit of suggesting *zētēmata*, and of putting down in writing the various solutions offered.[18] One can admit, following William J. Slater's invitation, that an important dimension of "academic life" at the Museum of Alexandria consisted in banquets, where philological problems, real or facetious, were discussed while drinking, and the solutions competed with one another in their ingeniousness. Some of Aristophanes of Byzantium's textual conjectures may have drawn their inspiration from those traditional questions.[19]

Plutarch and Athenaeus thus testify to the happy fortune that the Alexandrine model knew among private circles, where the symposium was the setting for erudite discussions, ordered around the questions offered to the sagaciousness of the audience.[20] Contrary to Plutarch's guests—to the most eclectic curiosity and to certain aspects that are closer to the Aristotelian tradition of "problems"—the deipnosophists remain within the field of literary and lexicographical erudition. Besides, it is significant that Athenaeus chose to organize his work on the basis of that operational principle. The *zētēsis* introduces us to the heart of his project and to the implications inherent in his enterprise; I shall underline three of them in order to close our journey: the relation to language; the particular regime of textuality specific to the *Deipnosophists*; and finally, the construction, within the work, of a reflexive knowledge, through which a culture tries to decipher itself.

---

[18] *Scholia ad Iliadem* 9.682 Erbse. See the discussion in Fraser 1972:2.471 n86.
[19] Slater 1982.
[20] Plutarch's *Banquet of the Seven Sages* also gives an important place to questions and *zētēsis*: see 150B–C, the discussion of the patronage of Dionysus *Lusios*, "the one who unties" but also "the one who finds solutions"; see also 151A–C, 152F–153F.

14

Words and Things

T HE MENTAL GYMNASTICS of the deipnosophists are not only a mechanism that produces and combines quotations indefinitely. Despite its playful character, it is not an end in itself. It plays an instrumental role in the constitution and the enrichment of a field of knowledge and, more generally, in a project that is at the same time social, ethical, and intellectual: through the multiplicity of its objects, the *zētēsis*, within Larensius' circle, aims to reconquer, to reactivate, and to preserve a cultural identity. Athenaeus' characters have made the choice, also very common in cultured Greek-speaking circles of the imperial era, of reactivating the cultural universe of the Greece of a given period, from Homer to the Hellenistic monarchies. The reference to a past that is definitely behind them poses the problem of the relation with the present, the time of the Roman Empire, the time of the banquet and of the statements that took place in it. The chronological and geographical gap and the changes that had taken place in the world order, with the Roman dominion over the Greek East, required a set of mediations that made it possible to recover that cultural universe and to immerse oneself in it. For Athenaeus and his characters it is the library that instead represents that mediation. It circumscribes an intellectual space where that culture is collected and preserved, in the two dimensions highlighted previously: on the one hand, the great literary, philosophical, and historical texts and, on the other, the texts that interpret, inventory, articulate, and construct objects from the repository of "primary sources": lexica, commentaries, and *hupomnēmata*.

To be Greek, to speak Greek, to want to play Greek, to study Greek in Rome at the end of the second century AD, were thus all things that involved recourse to the library as an essential source of knowledge on people, places, words, practices, beliefs, objects, and relations to the world. It was an essential but not exclusive source, since orality, rhetorical displays, school, rhapsodes and musicians (Larensius made use of both) also contribute to that cultural reactivation in the same way as objects, cooking recipes, table manners, and ways of life in society or conversation. Books remain, however, the privileged and most important source. They are at the same time a field of archaeological excavation and instruments of the deipnosophists, between the library of Larensius and their mental libraries. That work on the library is inseparable from a reflection on the practice of research itself, on the maintenance of the collection (whence Athenaeus' preoccupation with biblioteconomy), on the relevance of the questions and of the answers. And that reflection is collective, it unrolls under the control and in the light of the assessment of all the guests, it gives rise to controversies and debates on method.

An essential dimension of that cultural archaeology concerns the Greek language as such, and the relation of words to things. In doing this, the deipnosophists throw a critical and genealogical gaze on the language they use in their conversations, whether it is their mother tongue or a language of culture, as in the case of Larensius and of the other Romans present at the banquets. However, even those who speak Greek as a mother tongue are not content with the Greek spoken in their time. One of the functions of *zētēsis* is that of reconquering a past state of the language, or, more precisely, of constructing it, defining its rules, its semantics, its morphology, and its grammar. Indeed, their language does not correspond to the "common" Greek (the *koinē*) that was spoken in the imperial period, and it is actually questionable whether their language was ever spoken as such. The deipnosophists do indeed discuss the written literary language, the language of Attic poetry and prose, which can be reconstructed by putting together the rules and usage observed in some key author. Theirs is a language that has been reconstructed by the work of the grammarians, philologists, and lexicographers of Alexandria, but which also constitutes a relevant object of reflection for the rhetors and prose-writers of the Second Sophistic, in search of stylistic and linguistic norms.

Here I will limit myself to underlining the important implications of the linguistic question in the *Deipnosophists*. Three threads interweave: the inventory of words, the determination of their meaning and their form, and linguistic normativity, the latter tending to define not only the correct use of words, but also a linguistic norm that is only found in Atticist purism. Following those threads, Athenaeus' characters come and go between past and present, between written and oral language, between Greek and Latin.

As we have seen, one of Ulpian's obsessions consists in resituating the largest possible number of words within the usage of the ancients, to endow them, that is, with the authority of one or more quotations. "Where is it found?" is his favorite question, and his companions sometimes reproach him his narrow conception of *zētēsis*. That also earned him the surname of "hunter of words" (3.122c; 4.184a–b; 14.649b; 15.671f). All deipnosophists are hunters of books, and for that they root themselves in the bibliophile erudition that originated in the great Hellenistic libraries. Hunters of words collect more volatile objects, often from the books that they have gathered. Both groups are driven by a logic of accumulation and *sunagōgē*, and must work out ways that will help them master their collections. The catalogue (*pinax*) allows the mastery of a large quantity of books, manipulating and combining such "metadata" as the author's name and the work's title, and distributing them in sections that reflect the organization of literature and knowledge. As for the lexicon, it allows the ordering of the collection of words, for example in alphabetical order. However, just like the catalogue is not the library, the lexicon is not the language, even when it attempts to register the largest possible number of quotations, documenting the meaning and form of words in the best authors. Athenaeus' *Deipnosophists* is at the same time part book catalogue and part lexicon, but it dares to condense the library and, in a way, to reawaken language through the polyphony of quotations and the dialogue of the sophists.

Ulpian's "lexicography" presupposes a well-ordered library. It consists of running through that library following the thread provided by a keyword in order to collect its occurrences. Like a good hunter, Ulpian does not scorn rare and obscure words, as long as they are legitimized by a quotation. The taxonomies of objects and dishes that parade during the course of Larensius' banquets invite one to decline nouns, and often a ready reply or quotation on the part of another guest will in turn trigger new research. Most of the time, however, the answer to the question "Where is it found?" does not exhaust the curiosity of Ulpian and his companions. The literary sources and the stratification of lexica and commentaries are, in fact, the only mediation in order to reconstruct the link between words and things, to specify the meaning of words and define their form. The variations, the confusions, the mistakes of the lexicographers, the irremediable transition from orality to written discourse as the only horizon of the language's intelligibility: those factors make necessary an archaeology of the Greek language, where the critical use of lexica, the comparison between sources, the knowledge of *realia*, and, more generally, recourse to the whole range of literary equipment (grammar, etymology, philology), lead to inventorying variants and, if possible, putting an end to controversies.

For instance, what are *kudōnia*, the fruit that bear the name of a Cretan city? Quince apples, dictionaries tell us. But Athenaeus goes beyond that: "Nicander of Thyateira states that *kudōnia* are called *strouthia*, but he is wrong. Glaucides, on the contrary, states that the best fruit are the *kudōnia*, the *phaulia*, and the *strouthia*." There follows a series of quotations on *kudōnia* by Alcman, Cantharus, and Philemon (3.81c–d). The game, in this digression, consists in relocating the fruit within a typology, and in reconstructing its literary echoes. For cabbage as for quince apples. Another example is tripods: does Ulpian let himself get caught in the trap out of malice or out of ignorance? When one of the cynics calls the table a "tripod", Ulpian exclaims: "Where did you go and find that a table can be called a 'tripod'?" Impassive, the cynic answers with an accumulation of references that go from the *Marriage of Ceyx*, attributed to Hesiod, to Xenophon's *Anabasis* (2.49a–d).

For Athenaeus, the reconstruction of the meaning of words takes place exclusively within the library, with a closed horizon. It is done through the juxtaposition of lexicographical information and the play of literary quotations that serve to complete words, nuance them, contradict them, and, always, to contextualize them. Whether the subject is fish, birds, vegetables, wine cups, or flower crowns, Athenaeus remains in a universe of words: things are reflected in the mirror of literature, and it is that iridescent, and sometimes enigmatic, reflection that interests his characters. Indeed, the word hunt makes it possible to draw up taxonomies of objects, to generate lists of extracts, and to follow perpetually new paths within the library. Such a hunt involves an inventory of testimonia that document the presence of an object or an animal in Greek literature. In the list of birds, for example, we read under *porphuris*: "Callimachus in his *On Birds* claims that the *porphurion* should be distinguished from the *porphuris*, and he catalogues the two separately. He adds that the *porphurion* goes into dark places to eat so that it will not be observed by anyone. Indeed, it considers an enemy anyone who approaches its food. The *porphuris* is also mentioned by Aristophanes in the *Birds*. Ibicus calls some birds *lathiporphurides* [hidden *porphurides*]"; at this point, two quotations from Ibicus follow (9.388d–e). What attracts Athenaeus' interest? Certainly not that variety of bird, but the extracts from Callimachus and Ibicus that it allows him to mention; and also, the difference between *porphurion* and *porphuris*, and the curious food habits of the former, a curiosity that would not have been looked down upon by compilers of *mirabilia*.

The word-hunt is essential in preserving from oblivion entire segments of the Greek lexicon hidden in texts and glossaries. By re-establishing the link between words and things two opposing pitfalls are avoided: attributing different referents to synonyms, or bringing together as synonyms words that refer to different objects. Athenaeus repeatedly cites Speusippus' *Similar Things*,[1] where the pure pleasure of the sequence of words finds its expression, a witness to the creativity of the Greek language and its dialects in describing the same thing: the *rhaphanis*, the *gongulis*, the *rhaphus*, and the *anarrhīnon*, we are told, are all the same thing (9.369a–b). Our modern dictionaries, however,

---

[1]   See 7.323a–b, 327c–d.

teach us to find nuances: horseradish, radish, turnip, and cress, according to Bailly. Athenaeus adds: "No other vegetable resembles these except what today is known as *bounias*." (This is a sort of large turnip, says Bailly.) Since they do not have access to the vegetables as such, nor to any other type of object, only recourse to literary quotations can allow them to verify or invalidate the synonymy of words. It is a quotation from Callixeinus, who indicates that *thērikleion* and *karkhēsion* describe two different wine cups, and are not synonymous as Adaeus thought (11.471f–472a; see also 11.477b–d). Similarly, a quotation from Nicander's *Georgica* allows them to establish that the *khelīdonion* and the anemone are two different flowers (15.684d–e).

In return, the knowledge of local dialects makes it possible to enumerate the various names of the plum (2.49f), the lettuce (2.69b) and the wine cup (11.480f). For this, Athenaeus uses lexica like that of Nicander of Colophon (2.69b; 9.369a–b), or monographs, like the treatise of Apollas on the cities of the Peloponnese (9.369a). Putting the regional uses in sequence allows the collection of words to be enriched, and is part of the logic of accumulation that governs the entire text. In that listing of words and forms an imaginary Greece is deployed, where lexica and the entire library give the illusion that they can recover local particularities and manners of speech, in Rhodes, in Sicily, in Cyprus, or in Boeotia. An Alexandrine illusion indeed.

At the time of Athenaeus, Greek literature appeared to have been entirely indexed, its rare words redistributed in lexica, accompanied when necessary by contextual quotations and notes on their spelling and accent. The *Deipnosophists* testifies to the extent of the process initiated at the Library of Alexandria. Textual criticism, learned poetry, and erudite curiosity had fostered the development of lexicography, of collections of rare words found in texts of all periods and origins that were acquired by the Library. The words were classified, explained, grouped by theme and geographical origin. And already in Alexandria and Pergamon the question arose as to the usage of those words among the ancients, as well as the codification of the Attic dialect, even if grammarians like Istros, Eratosthenes, and Aristophanes of Byzantium did not prescribe its imitation as a literary language.[2]

Athenaeus is at the same time the heir and the continuator of that erudition. Lexica and collections of rare words were among his reference works and are plentifully cited: the *Glossai* by Seleucus, Nicander, Glaucon, Pamphilus, and Clitarchus, the *Cretan Glossai* by Hermon (perhaps the same grammarian as Hermonax), the *Attic Vocabulary* by Philemon, the *Regional Denominations* by Callimachus and his monograph *On Birds*, the *Lexica* by Dorotheus of Ascalon

---

[2] Broggiato 2000.

and Parthenius, collected among the historians, and obviously Philetas of Cos, whose enigmatic *Scattered Glossai* bring us back to the earliest era of Alexandrine erudition. All those lexica bring definitions, quotations, and grammatical notes that at times intertwine, complete each other, and contradict each other as other quotations are brought up by the sophists. When necessary, Athenaeus can turn a critical eye on those works and dig out their errors.[3] However, the compilations of dictionaries only make the labyrinth more complicated, giving rise to a process of unending accumulation.

Whether it is a question of flowers, breads, or fish, vegetables, cups, or musical instruments, the meaning and usage of words are incessantly investigated during the conversations of the deipnosophists. One episode seems particularly significant to me, and probably contains a key to the understanding of the work as a whole. In Book 9 Larensius suggests a subject of *zētēsis* to his guests: "What do you think the *tetrax* is?" (9.398b–c). The answer comes immediately: "A type (*eidos*) of bird." A grammarians' habit, adds Athenaeus, who are unable to answer anything but "a type of plant," "a type of stone," or "a type of bird." So Larensius produces a quotation from Aristophanes mentioning the *tetrax,* and then invites his guests to search their memories in their turn. Silence. "Since you cannot find anything, I will show you that bird." At that point a live *tetrax* in its cage is brought in—a souvenir of Larensius' time as procurator in Moesia (398e–f). The bird is described in detail: size, aspect, voice. The company marvels. The bird is then brought to the kitchen and a little later it is served to the guests, who compare its meat to that of the ostrich. "We feed on questions," Larensius had declared at the beginning of the episode. One can indeed wonder what the deipnosophists are eating in this case: a rare bird, the name of a bird, or the answer to an interesting question? Also, the display of the *tetrax* is there to compensate for the failings of memory and the silence of the library, to re-establish the link between words and things, to prevent the deipnosophists from going astray in the labyrinths of intertextuality.[4]

Preserving the form of words is an equally difficult achievement. The quotations often introduce observations relating to the spelling, accentuation, and gender of words. A dual tendency can be observed: on the one hand, to

---

[3] See for example the interesting discussion on the *Women of Thrace* (*Thrattai*), a variety of fish mentioned in Archippus' comedy *The Fishes*. Athenaeus recalls that in Book 108 of his collection of words, Dorotheus of Ascalon writes *thētta*. He then advances a double conjecture to explain the anomaly: either Dorotheus had an incorrect copy of the comedy, or he corrected the word because of its unusual character. Athenaeus refers the readers who wish to know more to the treatise he has devoted to Archippus' comedy (7.329b–e)

[4] The episode of the *mūma*, a mysterious dish announced as a subject of *zētēsis* by one of the cooks, can perhaps be interpreted in a similar way (14.658e).

indicate the changes in usages; on the other, to prescribe the correct norm. The quotations, however, testify to the possibilities of the language. For Sophocles, "thistle" is a noun that is sometimes feminine (*kunara*), sometimes masculine (*kunaros*) (2.70a). Thyme and oregano are found in the masculine, the feminine, and the neuter (2.68b–c). Similarly, in Attic, *skuphos*, the wine cup, can be masculine or neuter (9.498a).

However, the language does not dissolve into a kaleidoscope of variants. There are rules and norms. When Palamedes, another collector of words (*onomatologos*), on a day when he is served a dish of gazelle, expresses the following judgment: "The flesh of the *dorkones* is not unpleasant," Myrtilus answers him that one can only say *dorkades*, as attested by a quotation of Xenophon's *Anabasis* (9.397a). When one has the intention of bringing to new life the cultural universe of Hellenism through one's library and one's language, one ought to respect its grammar, which defines the rules of correct usage for the par excellence form of Greek, i.e. Attic. The deipnosophists do not hesitate, among themselves, to refresh each other's memory, be it on the reduplication of the lambda in female words ending in -*la* (7.305a), on the particular declension of the word "eel" in Attic (7.299a), or on the accentuation of the word *attagās*, where Attic usage goes against the general rule (9.388b).

The *zētēsis* of the deipnosophists is not limited to exhuming forgotten words and reciting long lists. In fact it also concentrates on rules and norms, and one of the issues at stake in the discussions (sometimes controversies) that take place within Larensius' circle is the reconstruction of Greek in its Attic form or in its most ancient usage. The love of archaism and Atticism are the two main characteristics of the Greek spoken by Ulpian (3.126e): a language that is acquired, controlled, and mastered to the point of affectation by that Syrian who has earned himself the nickname "Syro-Atticist" (3.126f), and does not touch a dish before having made sure that its name was or was not in use among the ancients, at the risk of slimming down to the point of fading away, like Philetas of Cos, the Alexandrine lexicographer whose body had been desiccated by the *zētēseis* (9.401d–e). Quoting an ancient or an Attic author can certify and authenticate. Can *tarīkhos* ("salted fish") also be masculine in Attic? Myrtilus produces the proof, a quotation from Cratinus (3.119b). Mobilizing everyone's memory, *zētēsis* makes it possible to prove the use of a word in ancient times, at least in the written and literary language, which is the only possible testimony for ancient linguistic usage. That sometimes leads into paradoxical situations. For example, the deipnosophists wonder about whether the ancients mention the lemon. Myrtilus thinks he has come across the word in Hegesander's *Notes*, but Plutarch proves him wrong. Aemilianus then quotes the treatise by Juba. Democritus cuts in: if the word *kitrion* cannot be found among the ancients, it is nevertheless without doubt that they knew the lemon, and that it is precisely the lemon that is the subject of a passage in Theophrastus' *Enquiries on Plants* (3.83a–c).

The use of the right words and correct forms makes it possible to re-establish contact and proximity with the world of the ancients. This proximity works on two levels: the grammatical mastery of Attic and of the nuances of its vocabulary enable new subtlety and pleasure in the reading of the classics; it also expresses itself, however, in the conscious and studied reuse of that language of culture, either in prose, in eloquence, or in the conversation itself. Indeed, that Hellenizing purism functions as a sign of recognition between readers and speakers, who share its demands and its codes. Those scholars assert their originality by distancing themselves from the usage of the current Greek language, the *koinē*, that has lost its rigor and purity.[5]

The choice of that language of culture involved a constant comparison with the vernacular Greek spoken in the imperial period. In a conversation circle such as that of Larensius one did not miss a chance to highlight the slips of the tongue and impurities that eventually penetrated the contributions of one or the other of the interlocutors. However, the effort and self-control required to speak in the same way as one wrote in the Athens of the fifth and the fourth century BC go hand-in-hand with a reflection on the evolution of the Greek language, on its characteristics of continuity and discontinuity. Indeed, some rare words remain in common use, like *thermokuamos*, describing a variety of broad bean (2.55e). Other words become specialized: today's usage, says Myrtilus, gives the name of *ornithēs* or *ornithia* to hens alone (9.373a). Ulpian has an infallible nose for words that are no longer in common use: "I know that *opsarion* ["fish"] cannot be found in any living author" (9.385b). To that, Myrtilus replies: "We say *opsarion*, and we count among the living" (385d), and follows this with a series of quotations from the comic poets Plato, Pherecrates, Philemon, and Menander, which was perhaps Ulpian's objective in the first place. Orality gives new life to forgotten words, and oral enunciation here confers upon the word the same ontological status that a bibliographical reference would have conferred to it.

Besides, it is impossible to ignore the situation of bilingualism in which all members of Larensius' circle found themselves, meeting in Rome and having to confront Latinity. Words and things move within a triangle, between Attic Greek, *koinē*, and Latin, and at times the deipnosophists take care to establish the equivalence between the language of the past and their contemporary Latin:

---

[5] Here Athenaeus reflects the polemics and the lexicographical and grammatical activity that accompanied that attempt to restore a past linguistic situation in reaction to the widespread use of the *koinē* even among scholars (Strabo, Galen, and so forth). For a general introduction see Anderson 1993, Chapter 4 ("Atticism and Antagonism"), and Swain 1996.

the *protogeustes* of today's Romans is perhaps the *protenthēs* of the Greeks of old, a "taster of dishes" (4.171c). The *cardus* of the Romans must be the equivalent of the *kaktos* of the Greeks, seeing that it is enough to substitute two letters in order to obtain the same word (2.70e–f). Epicharmus' *tellinē* may correspond to the *mitlos* (*mitulus*) of the Romans, that is to the mussel (3.85e). The *artos* of the Greeks corresponds to the Latin *panis* (3.111c). As for the citron, although it is true that the name is not found among the ancients, Pamphilus' lexicon nevertheless notes that the Romans call it *citrus* (3.85c).

Athenaeus mirrors the debates and linguistic choices of the cultured, Greek-speaking elites of the imperial period. If the Second Sophistic was preoccupied with revisiting the Greek heritage, it did not however limit itself to exploring its library and exploiting its deposits through the techniques of philology, commentary, and erudite compilation, as in Alexandria and Pergamon. In its project of cultural reactivation, performance constitutes an essential dimension, whether that means re-appropriating a lost language and making it resonate anew in the space of public discourse or private speech, or to put into play once again, in newly produced texts, the commonplaces, the beliefs, the categories, the values, and all the cultural, ethical, and philosophical stereotypes deduced from the classics, catalogued and analyzed in detail in rhetorical manuals. Athenaeus' *Deipnosophists*, where both orality and writing find their place, be it at the level of conversation or in systematically combing the library, participate doubly in that culture of performance.

However, in the mirror in which Athenaeus reflects the cultural preoccupations of his time one can also discern a certain distance as regards the excesses of linguistic purism and lexical erudition that can sink into oppressive affectation, or even into ridiculous obscurity. From that point of view Ulpian is an ambiguous figure: he plays an essential role by virtue of his investigations, his erudition, and his tireless search for the meaning of isolated words and of contextualized words. His preciosity, however, too often sinks into excess. When a wheat pudding is served to him, he asks for a spoon: "Give me a *mustilē*, because I do not have the intention of using the word *mustron*, which cannot be found in any author before our time" (3.126a). Athenaeus is enjoying himself. If Longinus was a living library, Ulpian is a living lexicon, who, in addition, eats the wheat pudding of the cynics with an Attic spoon, that is, a piece of bread that is used as a spoon. The most lively criticism is put forward by Cynulcus. When he asks to drink some *decocta*, a cold-water based sweet drink that was typically Roman, he provokes the anger of Ulpian, who accuses him of barbarism. Cynulcus answers that since he lives in Rome under the empire, he uses the local language, and invokes the precedent of ancient poets and prose-writers, who handled the purest Greek but at times used foreign words when they had entered common usage: Persian words, such as *parasangai* or *schoinos*, a measuring unit that was still in use, or Macedonian words. Besides, ancient authors took a less hard line than Ulpian, and sometimes had recourse to less constrained language, and even to improper words, as Cynulcus demonstrates through a series of quotations (3.121e–122d).

Language cannot remain enclosed in lexica, and the best authors know how to liberate themselves from rules. This is all the more true in Rome in the imperial period, where it is not always possible to speak like an Attic orator and ignore the ordinary language. Refusing to use Latin words leads to ridiculous verbal contortions, and to the creation of nouns that are just as foreign to classical usage: thus *phainolēs*, a neologism created by Ulpian to avoid using the Latin *paenula* as he is asking the slave for his cloak (3.97e). Cynulcus paints an entertaining picture of the "Ulpianist sophists" that can be encountered in the streets of Rome, with their ridiculous language, such as Pompeianus of Philadelphia, who thus addresses his slave while speaking of his new clothes: "Strombichides, bring me to the *palaestra* my 'unbearable' sandals and my 'useless' cloak. For after I have 'laced up my beard' I will go and chat with my friends" (3.97f–98a). In Ulpian's circles one prefers to speak of the *ipnolebēs* ("oven-cauldron") rather than the *miliarium* which serves to warm up the water (3.98c). Those creators of words revive the memory of other poets of the language, erudition-maniacs lost in the labyrinths of meaning, like the Sicilian Dionysius, who called the dens of mice "mysteries" because they protect (*tērei*) the mice (*mūs*) (98d); or Alexarchus, brother of Cassander, king of Macedonia, who founded Ouranopolis, "the city of the sky", and introduced there a particular language where the cock is called "cry of the morning" (*orthroboas*), and "barber" is called "shaver of men" (*brotokertēs*) (98e). Alexarchus had perhaps over-frequented the Alexandrine glossographers, but deep down Ulpian's temptation is the same: to invent words and to fantasize on their possible usage among the books of the library. Ulpian, *ho tōn onomatōn Daidalos*, the "Daedalus of words" (9.396a), the artisan who shapes and invents, the architect of the labyrinth, is also its prisoner.

15

The *Deipnosophists* as a Text
Genesis, Uses

IN THIS STRANGE PATH that associates banquets, a library, lexica, and insatiable scholars, we now need to ask what was the aim of the game. Is Athenaeus perhaps the victim of the most severe Alexandrine syndrome, that of a compilation mechanism destined to go indefinitely round in circles? Are the dialogue and its setup then nothing more than a miserable attempt to give literary coating to thousands of lexicographical entries and reading notes, or, put briefly, for the "cards" of an obsessive reader, which should never have left the shelves of his private library to enter the space of public circulation (*ekdosis*)? To count on the coherence of the text presupposes a reflection on Athenaeus' project and on the form of his work; this is precisely what we shall attempt to do now, after having brought to conclusion our "ethnographic" observation of Larensius' circle, investigated in its playful conviviality and its intellectual exercises.

The third book, of which we only have an abbreviated version, begins abruptly: "Since the grammarian Callimachus said that a great book is equal to a great evil" (3.72a). Is this the sigh of a learned copyist, or of the epitomizer himself, at the beginning of what appears like a grueling task? Or the *caveat* that an author addresses to himself, having a foreboding of the amplitude of his work? I would like to see in it an invitation to reflect on the *Deipnosophists* as a book, and also as a *mega biblion*, as a "great book".

How do things stand as to the nature of this book, its structure, its genesis, its uses, and the ways in which it was supposed to be read? What is the status of a book that reuses fragments of thousands of other books? To consider the *Deipnosophists* in the context of its genesis leads us once again to analyze the practices of the literati, which are the center of attention in Athenaeus' text itself, through the interaction of the members of Larensius' circle. Like Democritus (8.336d), Athenaeus is an expert on comic theater: his monograph on Archippus testifies to his taste for that literary genre. And, once again like Democritus,

Athenaeus uses the technique of the extract. One initial key to reading the *Deipnosophists* would be to consider the work as the collection of its author's reading notes, the map of his wanderings among books, whose linearity has been blown to pieces in favor of a different logic which is no longer bibliographical but thematic.[1] The reuse, quotation, paraphrase, and juxtaposition of fragments of texts of varying size are an essential component of Athenaeus' writing. The author (as we have seen) sometimes reuses long extracts from books in his work; such is the case of the quotation of the *On Alexandria* by Callixeinus of Rhodes, Lynceus' *Dinner-Party Letters,* and the treatise by Dioscorides of Tarsus that Athenaeus quotes or paraphrases in the course of his long digression on the way of life of Homeric heroes (1.8e ff.).

On the whole, however, Athenaeus' extracts are much shorter fragments, a few lines, or sometimes a single word. Taking notes during one's own readings can serve two different purposes: either one wants to extract from a book all the content and all the words that are noteworthy, all the facts worth being remembered for their surprising or enigmatic character; or one can have in mind the filtering of the extracted material according to a given question or writing project. That filtering operation can also be applied to a collection of extracts that was put together previously, or even to a lexicon. In that operation, which is characteristic of the literary activity of the Hellenistic and the imperial periods, and even beyond, the book is considered as a source of information and raw material that linear reading has the function of bringing together. Extraction enables the segmentation of those materials and their archiving on a level different from the original text. It certainly answers a preoccupation of ergonomic order, since extraction is selection, but also subdivision of a continuous text into elements that are independent, objectivized, mobile, and such that they lend themselves to any sort of new combination. The procedure also has intellectual effects, since decontextualization cannot happen without a form of recontextualization, which produces specific meanings: alphabetical order, thematic groupings, or the juxtaposition of various solutions brought to the same problem are so many forms of reorganization that produce knowledge and create poles of local coherence around an object or a question.

Gathering extracts from a text and keeping them in the order of succession they had in the original text means to epitomize, albeit in elliptical mode. Besides, that is the operation undertaken in Athenaeus' text itself. The form of compilation expresses the lack of satisfaction of a reader (or a group of readers), and in a way achieves a transformation of the reading protocol, a transformation

---

[1] One could compare the *Deipnosophists* with the treatise *On the Tranquillity of the Soul* 464F and 465A, which Plutarch states he composed on the basis of his collection of personal notes. See Dorandi 2000:27ff.

that dissociates content from form and the information from the letter of the text. The author of the epitome of the *Deipnosophists* has filtered the informative content of the text eliminating facts that were useless in his eyes, in this case a great number of bibliographic clarifications and the digressions linked to the dialogue of the deipnosophists. On the other hand, gathering extracts from a text, distributing them according to a different order and sometimes mixing them with extracts from other texts, results in the creation of a new text. The juxtaposition of heterogeneous statements, their reuse within a discursive line like Athenaeus' dialogue, produces specific meanings and constructs a new knowledge. The *Deipnosophists* produces a global knowledge that none of the reused quotations could have produced by itself as such. Such is the effect of the ordering of information in series, following a subject or a problem.

The particularity of Athenaeus lies in his not having taken compilation to its extreme stage, which would have consisted in suppressing from the quotation all the indicators of its initial context and author, and objectivizing the contents by paraphrasing or summarizing them. The indication of the bibliographic source has authenticating value, and anchors every quotation within the space of the library. It also poses, in a provocative way, the question of the relation with that library.

Modern commentators have evidently wondered about the amplitude of Athenaeus' readings: has he read all the texts he cites? Or, more precisely, are the quotations the result of his activity of *eklogē* practiced directly on the works? Or has Athenaeus used intermediate sources that themselves had already gathered quotations on the most disparate subjects? The search for Athenaeus' sources is a subject of *zētēsis* that would probably not have been scorned by Larensius' circle, and it is a subject that will continue to provide thesis subjects in universities for several generations still. However, using Athenaeus in order to reconstruct previous compilations that he may have cannibalized in silence, and of which practically nothing has come down to us, is something that belongs to the field of highly conjectural activity, and I shall not endeavor to proceed in that direction.[2] I shall, on the contrary, attempt to reformulate the problem. What implicitly underlies the *Quellenforschung* is a depreciative vision both of the author and of the discursive form and the intellectual project within which he inscribes himself. It is rather a perspective of accusation, since the techniques of philology bring to light the cannibalization of the works of others; a theft with aggravating circumstances, moreover, since apart from everything else, that way of proceeding shows remarkable intellectual laziness, the author

---

[2] At the end of the nineteenth century the German philologist F. Rudolph saw in the *Universal History* of Favorinus of Arelate the main source of both Athenaeus and Aelian. His reconstruction is now considered obsolete.

limiting himself to drawing from lexica and compilations, and then redistributing the materials and making them his own. Such an accusation, however, presupposes a mode of book circulation where the status of author is recognized and protected; an intellectual community with its rules and principles; and a specific status of the work as a personal intellectual creation.

Now how do things stand as to those reference works: lexica, collections of quotations, and thematic monographs bringing together the written sources concerning a given subject? They give access to textual materials that may have escaped the reader of the works in question, and a compiler like Athenaeus can, in theory, for the same authors, use his own reading notes and integrate them with this or that quotation provided by a lexicon, without necessarily mentioning the intermediate source. What is essential is the information thus gathered.

The *Deipnosophists* are a deconstructed library, cut into pieces that are then redistributed according to the thread of the meal and the *sumposion*. Those fragments go from the isolated word to the quotation of many dozens of verses. The lexica and compilations, which from the third century BC had also undertaken to sift through the library according to multiple grids, were Athenaeus' natural working instruments, and are, besides, often quoted as such. They individualize, select, and combine those quotations of varied origins; they read the classical authors at the first, second, and third degree; they create poles of local and thematic coherence by making the fragments interact and by making them instrumental to a project of cultural archaeology: compilation hides an activity that is properly literary and is a form of rewriting that can be traced both in the framing of the quotations (how do they start? and how do they end?) and in the modifications made to the letter and to the meaning of the texts. Those modifications can, on the one hand, be the result of the imprecision of memory, or of the mistakes introduced in the progressive stages of transcription of reading notes, from the tablets to the *hupomnēmata* and to the finished work. However, a careful reading also reveals a subtle and deliberate game by virtue of which Athenaeus modifies or changes the text of the fragments so as to better insert them within a thematic treatment.[3] That game reveals a real activity on the texts, both on the level of the selection of materials and on that of transcription and assemblage. The very project of Athenaeus would be meaningless if it were based in large part on one or more earlier collections—not to mention that an enterprise such as that would be insulting to Larensius, his bibliophile protector (assuming that we do not relegate Larensius to fiction).

---

[3] See the stimulating remarks by Pelling 2000, who invites us to re-examine the techniques and stylistic principles of writing and compilation.

A close reading of Athenaeus shows that in reality he very frequently mentions the indirect sources from which he gained access to a quotation of an ancient author. It is by multiplying the filters and sieves that he can put together his materials, and his practice of compilation may reflect the working techniques of his characters. An indirect quotation also presents an intellectual, almost aesthetic interest: it adds a diachronic dimension to the vast synchronic network of connections between fragments of text. It inscribes them in a tradition, in chains of transmission, and it inscribes itself in the continuity of an intellectual practice that is attested by the lexicographers, the scholars, and the grammarians of the past, but also by all the great readers, be they philosophers, historians, or exegetes. It doubly proves the culture of the compiler, who not only extracts materials from the texts he has at his disposal, but knows where to look for quotations of texts to which he has no direct access, since he knows the "basic instruments" of literary activity: "Those iambic verses have been quoted by Didymus and by Pamphilus" (11.487c). And finally, the indirect quotation constitutes an interesting object in itself, and offers suggestive material to the contemporary reader for the study of text transmission. What does it mean to read Empedocles through a quotation by Theophrastus (10.423f)? Or Anacreon through Simmias (11.472e)? What does it mean to read an iambic composition by Hipponax through Lysanias and his work *The Iambic Poets* (7.304a–b), or through Pamphilus' lexicon (2.69d), or Hermippus' monograph *Hipponax* (7.327b)? Or Asius through Duris (12.525e)? Or to come to an entry of Theodorus' *Attic Glossary* thanks to Pamphilus' lexicon (15.677b)? Even when books had become impossible to find, the indirect tradition still conveyed precious fragments; Athenaeus himself participates in that historical process.

So how do things stand with the *Deipnosophists* as a text? Is it a disorderly accumulation of reading notes, roughly grouped by theme: vegetables, breads, fish, wine cups, crowns, and so on? Certainly not. Athenaeus' characters play an important part in the construction of the text and in its thematic structuring. After all, they are the ones who quote and explore their mental libraries, bringing innumerable quotations out of them. Their dialogue rules, controls the flow of quotations, and defines their relevance, their appropriateness. That which from time to time reveals itself as appropriate in the course of the conversation, *kairos*, determines the distribution of the extracts.[4] Athenaeus' text is constructed and articulated: that is demonstrated by the many internal cross-references which establish anaphoric ("we have seen that...") or cataphoric ("we will see that...") connections within a book or from one book to another. The mention of those connections is meaningful both within the dialogue of the deipnosophists, who

---

[4]   See 3.110a; 4.134c, 162a; 8.348d; 13.564f–565a, 579d–e; 14.622d.

are in that way required to master within their memory everything that has been said (their mental libraries become enriched not only with what they have read and extracted from books, but also what they have heard), and in relation to the reading of the work itself. Timocrates, who listens to Athenaeus' account, is here a substitute for the reader, and all those references delineate the way in which to use the *Deipnosophists* as a text, its ergonomy.

Indeed, those connections testify to a double preoccupation: that of an author and of the characters he sets up, desiring to put into order a considerable mass of discontinuous, heterogeneous, and decontextualized textual materials, and that of the reader, who will have to trace his itineraries within the work. It is in that sense that Athenaeus is presented, from the very beginning of the work, as the steward (*oikonomos*) of the text (1.1b). For the author, as for the reader, memory is the determining factor, because the internal anaphoric and cataphoric references are not cross-references like the ones we encounter in our books with numbered pages but are points of reference that are relative and refer backwards or forwards from the passage being read. It is not expressed precisely whether that will involve a move backwards or forwards, a move of some few lines or of several rolls.[5]

Athenaeus' composition technique cannot be dissociated from the ways in which his text is appropriated. To which readers is it addressed? And for what use? Was it intended for Athenaeus' private use? Was it meant to circulate outside Larensius' circle?[6] And what was its link with Larensius? Was the work perhaps built in the image of his library of ancient Greek books, condensed, exploited, run through from every direction?

A careful look at the composition of the text itself reveals a certain formal heterogeneity: indeed, Athenaeus uses different discursive genres, different regimes of textuality, such as comic or Platonic dialogue, dissertation, lexical lemmata, lists, or the simple juxtaposition of extracts. One can see one of the characteristic traits of a text marked by diversity and variety (*poikilia*), both in theme and in form; and perhaps one can also see the traces of the genesis of the work, having been pieced together little-by-little from the materials found while reading, and traces of the first editorial processing of specific subjects. The *Deipnosophists* would then be not only a library, but also a scholar's small study, where all the stages of his work are preserved. That heterogeneity, however,

---

[5] For example, 9.401f–402a refers to 4.128a; 10.415d refers to 4.144f; 10.453c–e to 7.276a; 11.496a to 3.125f; 12.543b to 4.168d; 14.615a to 4.261c. There are also many anaphoric and cataphoric references within a single book.

[6] The absence of papyrological attestations, the rareness of quotations from Athenaeus in later authors, and, finally, the manuscript tradition itself, which is based on the Codex Marcianus 447 and on its epitome, suggests that Athenaeus' work did not circulate widely.

also adapts itself to the nature of the materials used and to the subjects tackled, some of which lend themselves to a continuous discussion, others to a catalogue bound to be perpetually increased, others still to polemics, and to the necessary formulation of different points of view. For the reader, this results in different approaches to the text, from continuous reading to ad hoc consultation.

For example, the first book, only preserved in the epitome, contains a whole treatise built into it, with its own title, *On the Way of Life of Homer's Heroes* (1.8e and 24b). Does Athenaeus reuse the treatise by Dioscorides of Tarsus, as the *Suda* suggests? Or is it a summary and a set of reading notes? Either way, we are here dealing with a treatise that is thematically coherent and autonomous, which could have existed independently on a roll of papyrus. Some extended speeches of the deipnosophists are also close to a *hupomnēma*. Plutarch, for example, treats of the question of parasites (6.234c–248c); he is followed by Democritus with a long talk on flatterers (6.248c–262b). In both cases we are dealing with a continuous exposition, a real oral dissertation, where the orator discusses the materials he has collected in his memory. Those accounts can also constitute independent treatises, and it is probable that they were written as such before they were reused within the dialogue.[7]

For the lists, Athenaeus sometimes but not always adopts the principle of alphabetical order. Those lists can be minimalistic, like the catalogue of breads, put together from various glossographers, where the name is accompanied by the bibliographic sources and by a brief definition (3.114b). At times, they allow him to stock up a large quantity of other information. The text then becomes a glossary: every entry opens with a word, then brings together all the information concerning it. The list of fish offers a particularly interesting example, because the narrator chooses to reorganize the conversations of the deipnosophists within an alphabetical list, so that Timocrates can memorize them more easily (7.277b–c). In the logic of the narration, that choice recalls once again those performances of combinatorial memory that can redistribute into an alphabetical list the materials memorized during a conversation, filtering out a certain number of facts, such as the name of the interlocutors.[8] This series of cards in alphabetical order, however, corresponds most probably to the original editorial phase, the phase, that is, when Athenaeus collected his materials, finding support in lexica and in his extracts; that was a way of proceeding that

---

[7]   See also, at 11.487f–494b, the long discussion concerning Nestor's cup, which also takes the form of a dissertation and which moreover is largely dependent, in this case, on the treatise by Asclepiades of Myrlea.

[8]   See also 14.616e, where Athenaeus, as he is speaking to Timocrates, decides to bring together in a single account everything that has been said by the deipnosophists on the pastimes of the banquet, without respecting the order of succession of the conversations or the names of the interlocutors.

lent itself to the progressive enrichment of his database, from discovery to discovery and from reading to reading, until it found itself embedded in Book 7 of the *Deipnosophists*. In Book 2 we find a lexicographical sequence concerning all the dishes eaten during the initial phase of the banquet (2.51b–71f), and in Book 14 (643e ff.) a list of sweets. Neither one nor the other are in alphabetical order. Such lists can be used for the ordering of the most disparate forms of information: etymology, synonyms, morphology, usage, quotations, grammatical annotation, and so forth, juxtaposed without having been articulated. The entries create poles of local coherence, collecting the highest possible number of facts on a particular theme or topic. On that same model Athenaeus also proposes a list of courtesans (13.583d–e ff.).

Finally, this also poses the question of the uses of the text, of its reading protocols. Was it a work that was to be read continuously, following the thread of the banquet and the symposium, and the unfolding of the meeting from the beginning to end? Was it a dialogue, between a comedy and a conversation of wise men, which made it possible to follow the interaction of characters with strong personalities, their mood changes and their witticisms? Or were the *Deipnosophists* a vast repertory of materials meant to be reconfigured and extracted, so as to be integrated into new *hupomnēmata*?[9] Or was it, on the contrary, an immense collection of reading notes intended to be memorized and reused orally in other literary banquets? Or a *summa docta*, designed for ad hoc consultation by whoever mastered its structure and its thematic progression, in search of a word, an explanation, the treatment of a problem?[10]

Those are the many forms of appropriation of this oceanic work, which now lead us to consider navigation as a structural key and as the essential principle in reading it.

---

[9] In the fourth century, the sophist Sopatrus of Apamea, a disciple of Iamblichus, collected in twelve books all the extracts drawn from his readings. In the first book, in particular, he had collected the notes extracted from Athenaeus' *Deipnosophists*. The books that follow testify to the use of other such collections: the *Epitomai* by Pamphila, the *Universal History* by Favorinus, the *Miscellaneous Notes* by Aristoxenus, the *Lives of the Philosophers* by Diogenes Laertius, and so on. Photius has preserved a detailed summary of Sopatrus' collection (*Bibliotheca*, cod. 161).

[10] The answer to those questions is not obvious, and would require a general inquiry into the modes of circulation of texts written in erudite and literary circles. Pliny the Elder was offered four hundred thousand sesterces for his hundred and sixty rolls of reading notes (Pliny the Younger, *Letters* 3.5.17). See also Aulus Gellius, *Attic Nights* 14.6.

16

The Web of Athenaeus
The Art of Weaving Links

"**E**VERY TIME WE MEET, my friend Timocrates, you repeatedly ask me what was said at the meetings of the deipnosophists, thinking that we discover new things..." That is the opening to Book 6 (222a). In Book 14, Athenaeus once again mentions the ever new speeches that took place within Larensius' circles (613c–d), and at the beginning of Book 15, turning to his listener, he mentions the extreme difficulty of his task, which consists in "recalling all the things that were said so often in these banquets, attended with such zeal, not only because of the diversity, but also because of the similarity, of the discoveries made there time and again" (665a).

What were the novelties discovered in those meetings?[1] Surely it was neither the latest gossip about Roman high society, nor the court rumors. The formulation is paradoxical: indeed, what novelty can ever come out of the conversations of lovers of ancient Greek books, which perpetuate the rite of the Attic *sumposion*? And what does Athenaeus mean when he mentions the *poikilia* and the *homoiotēs*, the diversity and the similarity, of the speeches held at the *domus* of Larensius?

The library (that of Larensius; that of Athenaeus; that which every deipnosophist bears imprinted in his memory) seems to me to be the key to this paradox. From that space that is shared, mastered, and mapped by the catalogues and the erudition of the Hellenistic era, the rule of the game is to produce the *kainon*, to bring out something new and original from this intellectual and linguistic space of identity, and to reawaken those deposits of words and knowledge by way of paradoxical paths and unexpected explanations. The order of the library, the subdivisions of Callimachus' *Pinakes*, the topography of literary genres and fields of knowledge, the attribution of authors to those genres and

---

[1] See also Braund 2000b:18.

fields, but also to a geographical space and a period, the bibliographical meta-data that enable the identification of books by cross-checking the criteria (title, number of books, incipit): all this contributes to structuring a mental space that may have imitated the compartments of material libraries. However, the *Deipnosophists* is not the map of that space, and Athenaeus did not choose, like a new Callimachus, to write the well-ordered catalogue of Larensius' library. For him, as for his characters, the most important thing consists in passing through that space, in travelling inside it, in the tracing of itineraries that are both personal and part of a social game at the same time.

A project of that sort presupposed two conditions. The first is the construction of a complex, multidimensional space, where it is possible to move on several levels, horizontally and vertically, between the primary and the secondary literature, between literary genres, between books, and between extracts and words. If we admit that bibliographic competence and grammatical culture provided each of those scholars with a mental satellite navigation system that allowed him to move into all recesses of the library without ever losing sight of his own position within a coherent general framework, then the library could be deconstructed, apportioned into separate units, into fragments, into words. Second condition: that fragmented library is a space of travel, where the only imperative consists in never stopping and in multiplying the connections, in tracing an itinerary that connects the largest possible number of textual elements, which makes it possible to take the longest route to the destination, if possible, between poles that are extremely far from each other.

From that perspective, rather than the account of a banquet, Athenaeus' work should be the story of a fascinating round of a party game. The rule could be formulated as follows: it is suggested to—or imposed upon—each player to localize a specific spot in the library (an author, a text), for example in the form of a question by Ulpian, a question in its turn related to one of the dishes or one of the incidents of the banquet, or even with a word pronounced by the previous player. The player must then locate his starting point (that is the meaning of Ulpian's question: "Where can it be found?") and, from that point, connect between them the highest possible number of other textual points. The quotations are like pawns with which the player marks the point of his itinerary as it progresses within the library.[2] If the novice players were asked to do simple things, like quoting the names of the heads of the Achaeans or the Trojans, or of the cities of Europe or Asia (10.457e–f), the expert players, which is what Athenaeus' characters are, look for sophisticated challenges, and

---

[2]   The process of quotation is defined as a "path": 4.164d: *hexēs katadramontos*. Elsewhere it is also possible to note the presence of the vocabulary of digression: *parexēben* (10.429f).

suggest complicated research subjects (*zētēseis*) to each other, sometimes forbidding recourse to the most obvious sources (as noted, Myrtilus asks Ulpian to avoid using a source known to everyone: 15.676e–f). It could be said that a good subject is one that allows the longest transversal route. Which raises the question, for the players as for the author and the reader, of where to put an end to the game, which in turn raises the possibility that it may never be complete. If the starting point is set, where does one stop, and how?

The games seem to have two inescapable rules. The first consists in the fact that the concatenation of quotations or of words must be governed by the principle of relevance. Admittedly, this principle is interpreted broadly and allows an open choice of associative strategies: by analogy, bibliographic source, theme or keywords, antithesis, mutual rectification, the successive addition of clarifications, alphabetical order, and so forth.[3] One example among others: the discussion concerning the musical instrument called *sambukē* leads into the mention of war machines, since one of them bears the same name (14.633f–634a). Some words can thus be semantic crossroads, allowing for the channeling of the conversation in various directions. From that point of view, it is important to master the quotations that can reveal themselves to be relevant to several subjects, since they make these sorts of thematic bifurcations possible (3.107b). The virtuosity of Athenaeus' characters consists in relating independent words or fragments of texts to one another, and in establishing in this way the largest possible number of stages between a start and end point, before passing the ball to the next player. The main goal lies perhaps less in the quotations that are produced (any well-trained slave was capable of that), than in the intellectual process that connects them. The second rule consists in the fact that those routes have to remain within the library, that is within the space of what is said, what can be said, what is attested. In this game, nothing is said without the production of witnesses or guarantors. The bibliographic reference has the value of an authenticator, and it is indispensible for the game to be valid. Included in the rule of the game: one can cite an author either because one has read him in person, or on the basis of a previous quotation taken up by a lexicographer or a compiler—a small concession that enables a considerable increase of the repertory of relevant quotations.

This game is also the compositional principle of the work of Athenaeus himself. The text of the *Deipnosophists* could be considered as the chronohistory of those navigations, of that game. Athenaeus collects those fragments of itinerary one after another, the sum of which actually makes possible a complete

---

[3] On the importance of analogy and digression as factors in the articulation of the quotations in the *Deipnosophists*, see Pelling 2000. See also the discussion in Anderson 1974:2181ff: "Athenaeus exhibits an almost Ovidian ingenuity in managing the transitions."

tour of the library. This, then, is what the originality of his project consists in: in having attempted to pin down the flow, the connections made by memory, those continuous movements and those mental associations; in having made of the mobility and dynamics the compositional principle of a text, which has prevented an immense collection of reading notes from sinking into chaos.

Let us give one example among a thousand others: "Heliodorus says that Antiochus Epiphanes, whom Polybius refers to as Epimanes because of his conduct, had the water of the fountain of Antioch mixed with wine: this is what the Phrygian Midas had done, says Theopompus [...]. According to Bion, the spring is common to the Maedes and to the Paeonians, and it is called Inna. Staphylus says that Melampus was the first to mix wine with water. Pleistonicus claims that water is also better for the digestion than wine" (2.45c). In a few lines seven authors are cited, and a single thread links water and wine; the whole seasoned with parentheses (Polybius interrupts Heliodorus), with geographical clarifications (Bion on the fountain), with a parallel (Theopompus), with a reference to the tradition of inventions and medical literature.

Some itineraries can run through a given author in a sequence of quotations: Poseidonius (4.151e ff.; 6.246c–d), Theopompus (6.166d–167a) or Demetrius of Scepsis (4.173f–174a). Others can take their cue from an analogy with the preceding statement: the treatment given by Cynulcus to the feast of the *Phagēsia* inspires Plutarch to take up the feast of the *Lagunophoria* in Alexandria, *kata to homoion* (7.276a). Still others proceed by concentric movements or by measuring distance radially from a single word. Or they have recourse to the disagreement of sources concerning a given question: the vine was invented in Olympia, claims Theopompus. Hellanicus says it was in an Egyptian city. Dio the Academic adds that this is the cause of the the Egyptians' love of wine and drinking. And Aristotle adds that drunks fall on their face... (1.34a–b).

So, to return to the dialogue between Athenaeus and Timocrates, where does the "novelty" of the subjects treated in the conversations of the deipnosophists lie? Admitting that each of their meetings traced a new itinerary within the library, based on the playful and interactive pattern that we imagine, the result could then be the account of a new trip every time, with stops, points of view, unexpected meetings, within a cultural space nevertheless well-provided with points of reference. A travel account that, for example, made it possible to revisit Strabo's *Geography*, perhaps by means of a secondary source, so as to extract from it information on the city of Saxitania, famous for its salted fish (3.121a).[4] Or to show how even an author of primary importance like Polybius

---

[4] It would be interesting to develop the parallel between the figures of the cooks, both in the quotations from comedy and when they speak during the course of the banquet, and the

can bring, to those who know how to read him, an interesting contribution to the moral, material, and political archaeology of the culture of the symposium.[5] The *Deipnosophists* that we read today is but one configuration among other possible ones for the same subject, but also, possibly, for other subjects (what results would Athenaeus' "method" yield if applied to subjects like art, the gods, animals, war, the city...?).

The contemporary category of hypertext can help us understand the status of Athenaeus' text, and the nature and purpose of the intellectual operations that produced it. Hypertext can be defined as a writing technique and as a reading technique at the same time. Both rely on itineraries, within one or several texts, that do not respect the linearity and continuity of writing, but establish links between spatially disjointed fragments or units of meaning. The links can be predefined by the author—the possibility of choice for the user is in this case limited—or they can be established by the reader himself, as a function of, for example, a specific intellectual project, or of a search for information. The best example of a hypertext is a standard webpage, on the present-day internet, where a certain number of connections can guide the reader to other pages, in a sort of arborescence of the document, or even to an infinite number of other documents, physically independent, but such that they can be put in relation with each other through the common thread of a keyword, a common theme, or of various degrees of logical or narrative presupposition.[6]

Of course, today the *Deipnosophists* is presented as a continuous and linear text, at least on a formal level. Yet the work in its complexity corresponds to a hypertextual trip through the space of the library, since the game of the deipnosophists consists in connecting between them hundreds of independent words and fragments of texts, in juxtaposing them and putting them in series, in passing from one to another. If that practice is the equivalent of an oral mnemotechnical performance, it is also the foundation of the discursive form chosen by Athenaeus, a complex redistribution of reading notes that follow the series of courses and of pastimes of a banquet. One could object that fixed in this way in a sequence of fifteen books, the text no longer presents the dynamic mobility that is constitutive of hypertext. However, all the indicators

---

deipnosophists. Indeed, both have the task of producing "novelty" with respect to their predecessors: 9.405d.

[5] On this question I am entirely in line with F. Walbank, "Athenaeus and Polybius," in *Athenaeus and his World*, 161–69, who shows how Athenaeus is not interested in the central theme of Polybius' work (the conquest of the *oikoumenē* by the Romans), and that instead, his quotations are the result of an original *eklogē* conducted directly on the text in search of materials relevant to his project.

[6] In the perspective of the history of the book and of writing practices, I believe the best introduction to these questions to be Bolter 1991.

of anaphoric and cataphoric references that link together separate parts of the work testify that the reader was invited to navigate upstream and downstream, to break the linearity of his path. Besides, Athenaeus provides a hypertext for the reader, or, more exactly, a chronohistory of his navigations, with all the textual places he has passed through successively within the library. Finally, one can wonder whether the work in itself required a linear reading or, on the contrary, favored ad hoc and discontinuous consultation, depending on, for instance, some particular thematic curiosity, or on the need to collect materials for a writing project.

17

The Epitome of the World

THE *DEIPNOSOPHISTS* CRYSTALLIZES a fluid chain of texts, fragments, and words, connected by the memory threads of a circle of literati and, ultimately, by the memory of Athenaeus himself. A double logic can be recognized in this, namely a centrifugal and a centripetal logic. By bringing together a vast complex of reading notes, the *Deipnosophists* condenses the library until it has reduced it to the size of a work in fifteen books. That size makes it possible to control it, even while it reflects, at the same time, its wealth, its *poikilia*, the infinite discoveries that can be made within it. The mastery of Athenaeus' work is not incompatible with the pleasure of losing oneself in it, of tracing new itineraries within it, or even of enriching it with new quotations.

The epitome of the first book preserves a strange digression (1.20b–c):

> Definition. He says that Rome is a city of the world. He also states that one would not be far off the mark if one said that the city of Rome is a "synthesis" (*epitomē*) of the inhabited world; it is thus possible in it to see at the same time all cities, and the greatest part of them with their own particularities, like the "city of gold" of the Alexandrians, "the beautiful city" of the Antiochenes, "the wonderful city" of the Nicomedians, and "the most splendid of all cities that Zeus illuminates", I mean Athens. An entire day would not suffice to count the cities included in the heavenly city of the Romans, Rome, but I would need all the days there are in the entire year, that is how many they are. Indeed entire peoples, all together, live here, like the Cappadocians, the Scythians, the Pontians, and many others.

Rome has become a universal city, where the entire *oikoumenē* is summarized. Rome makes it possible to see all of the world's cities through a synoptic gaze, and to discover the great Hellenistic *mētropoleis* together with the gem of the entire Greek world, Athens, and with the peripheral peoples. Admittedly, this digression recalls analogous cases in the epideictic rhetoric of the Second Sophistic, where praises of imperial Rome similar to this one were frequent. Yet in this paraphrase, perhaps truncated by the compiler, several elements are present that resonate with Athenaeus' text and project.

That synoptic gaze upon a condensed world, of which one sees the peoples and the cities, conjures up a cartographic metaphor. However, Rome is also the place where the Greek world is condensed, from the cultural capitals of the Hellenistic period—Alexandria first and foremost—to the Athenian core which was its inspiring source. Rome as a heavenly city (*ouranopolis*) can recall Alexarchus' politico-linguistic utopia: Rome as Babel, the place where all languages are spoken; or the paradigm of the universal city, in the terms in which it was delineated by the Stoics in particular. The itinerary that leads from the Greek East to the heart of the Empire is the same one that leads from the libraries of Athens, Alexandria, or Pergamon to that of Larensius in Rome. In the same way that the *oikoumenē* is condensed in the city par excellence, classical Hellenism and the layers of Hellenistic erudition have come to meet in Larensius' library. His table, moreover, sees the passage of the most refined dishes and foods, and it also condenses the best that the *oikoumenē* has to offer to gourmets. This high official also participates in the Roman utopia, since by virtue of his munificence he brings Lusitania to Rome (8.331b–c).

This "epitome of the inhabited world" is perhaps a reading key to the *Deipnosophists*. Just as Rome sees all cities and all peoples of the world condense in its space, so the library condensed in Athenaeus' text allows one not only to move through all the books that it contains, but also through the *oikoumenē*; to travel, to trace infinite itineraries, without ever coming out of a Roman *domus*. Larensius' circle is at the center of the world. That world, in turn, is composed of Greek and Roman scholars who come from the most diverse regions and who unite Roman and the Greek worlds, East and West, in the same ritual of conviviality. Larensius, Athenaeus tells us, turned Rome into the fatherland of all his guests (1.3c).

Dionysius the Periegete, at the time of Hadrian, from Alexandria, made the effort of describing the *oikoumenē* in a poem of several hundred verses; Pausanias wrote a *Periegesis of Greece* with the intention of saving the memory of its noteworthy monuments and of the stories associated with them. As for Athenaeus, he has chosen to write the *periēgēsis* of a library.[1] In this, he participates in the project of collection, salvage, and condensation of knowledge and memory that are characteristic of the Second Sophistic, but he also manifests an

---

[1] Anderson 1974:2178 also underlines this geographical dimension and evokes a "culinary Pausanias."

entirely Alexandrine obsession. His work testifies to the fact that a library makes it possible to travel, to run through the *oikoumenē*, just like a geographical map or a *periēgēsis*. Besides, Dionysius, Pausanias, and Athenaeus have in common the fact of travelling both in time and in space: the world of Odysseus or of the Argonauts, the monuments and inscriptions of classical Greece, the language and the culture of a Greek world that was becoming increasingly distant, are the subjects of their research, and their trips are also a process of *anamnēsis*.

The deipnosophists also employ a geographical horizon, and travel freely on that geographical map, unwinding the thread of words and quotations. The menus of the banquets can indeed lead to Sicily, to Sybaris, to Chios (1.25e–f). The wine list invites one to a *periēgēsis* of Italy, especially when the task of drawing it up falls to the physician Galen (1.26c). The evocation of famous banquets, whether those of kings, cities, or peoples, unravels a thread that leads the reader from Cilicia to Athens, then to Thebes, Arcadia, Naucratis, and Egypt, to the Galatians, the Thracians, the Celts, the Parthians, the Etruscans, the Indians, the Germans, the Campanians, and the Romans (4.147e–153f). When the moment comes to make the *periēgēsis* of peoples who have become famous by virtue of their *truphē*, Athenaeus invites us on another trip, in which we meet the Persians, the Medes, the Lydians, the Etruscans, the Sicilians, the Sybarites, the people of Croton and Tarentum, the Iapygians, the Iberians, the people of Massilia, and which after some stops in Magna Graecia leads us to the Scythians, the Syrians, the Lycians, and many others, until a provisional destination, Cumae, is reached (12.513e–528e). Ham brings us to Gaul, Cibyra, Lycia, and Spain (14.657e), while the name of the plum in a quotation from Clearchus links Rhodes and Sicily (2.49f). The cabbage, as we have seen, is also a good subject for travel: Eretria, Cumae, Rhodes, Cnidus, Ephesus, Alexandria (9.369e–f). The *Deipnosophists* also includes geographies of fish, of peoples with great drinkers (10.442a–443c), of drinking manners (9.463e–f), and so forth.

Athenaeus' project thus joins with that of Archestratus, the plentifully cited author of the *Gastrologia*, who "for love of pleasure toured the world and the seas" (7.278d) in search of everything that could satisfy "the belly and the parts below the belly" (3.116f). "Like those authors of Travels and Voyages, he aims to expound accurately 'wherever can be found any food and any drink that is most delicious'" (7.278d). In this way, Archestratus, that periegete of cuisine, takes us on a tour of Italy (7.294a).[2]

Motionless, the reader can travel, he who lets himself be transported by compilations from the interior of the library. When one considers this theme of the condensation of the world, which like a geographical map enables all

---

[2]   On this author see Olson and Sens 2000.

possible routes, strange correspondences establish themselves, explaining Athenaeus' project: correspondences between Rome and Alexandria, between the procession of Ptolemy Philadelphus (also a form of epitome of the world: 5.201d–e) and Larensius' table, between the banquets and the library, between the *truphē* of Polycrates, tyrant of Samos and great book collector (1.3a), who brings to his table dishes of every provenance—Epirus, Scyros, Miletus, Sicily (12.540c)—and Athenaeus, whose erudite bulimia and frenzy of accumulation belong to the field of spiritual *truphē*.

18

When a Culture Reflects on Itself

Tʜᴇ ᴡᴏʀᴋ ᴏғ Aᴛʜᴇɴᴀᴇᴜs would thus be a *periodos tēs bibliothēkēs*, a "tour of the library", perhaps the library of Larensius, but certainly also that of memory, and also the ideal library whose reconstruction is enabled by textual tradition, direct and indirect. That trip does not link the books between them but creates a multiplicity of links between the places that compose them: factual information, words, quotations. By weaving that fabric, Athenaeus dismantles the compartmentalized structure of the library, which fixes every text within a book and preserves its formal and intellectual autonomy and coherence.

The comparison with the tradition of *periēgēseis*, however, is only partially valid. If it is indeed true that the point is to move methodically inside a confined space so as to circumscribe and master it, that route adopts points of view that are placed on different levels, succeed each other, and proceed on the basis of changes in scale that lead, like in Ptolemy, from topography to geography and from the local to the global. Those changes in scale define a number of reading protocols. The *Deipnosophists* could be described metaphorically as a library that can be visited thanks to a helicoidal gallery, which allows one to go up little by little and to vary one's point of view on the central space, with the only difference that this variation does not correspond to a compositional principle of the text that will lead, in sequence, from bottom to top, but to a way of reading the text, where meaning is constructed, structured and hierarchized as the work is run through.

The architecture of the Solomon R. Guggenheim Museum in New York, created by Frank Lloyd Wright, could be the material version of that mental device, which seems to me to demonstrate the intention and effect of Athenaeus' text, and, for the modern reader, a key to its decipherment: [see Figure 1]

At the ground level of this device is the library of ancient Greek books, which preserves a heritage of culture and language, the space of travel and navigation, within which one moves by activating analogical links between countless textual loci, between words, between quotations that have been chosen

Fourth Level Mirror culture reflects on itself
Third Level Here and now:
   Rome, late second century AD
Second Level Metaliterature:
   sieve, magnifying glass, filters
First Level Bibliographical structuring
   of the library
Ground Level The library as a space of
   navigation

Figure 1

in the course of readings. As one begins to walk up the helicoidal ramp, one progressively gains height, and the library appears in its globality, but also with its internal partitions: that first level is that of Hellenistic bibliographic science, which organizes, subdivides, classifies, and identifies.

At the level immediately above that, and with one's gaze still turned to the library, the highlights of metaliterature become apparent, namely all those works of the Hellenistic and imperial periods—commentaries, lexica, monographs of literary history, and erudite collections—that have exploited classical literature and have become integrated in their turn within the collections. That metaliterature fulfills several functions for Athenaeus' text. First of all it plays the role of a sieve, through which scholars have passed classical Greek literature and language with the aim of collecting words, information, and quotations on every possible subject, or almost. The materials thus collected are generally classified and set so as to be used by readers wishing to have quick access to a given type of documentation without having to explore the entire library in person. Several successive levels of compilation can redistribute and interpolate those objects of knowledge, sometimes mixing them with complementary materials directly extracted from the original sources, sometimes filtering them, reorganizing them, distorting them—both in their letter and in their bibliographic identity or in their meaning. In its time, Athenaeus' *Deipnosophists* occupied the summit of the pyramid, but has since been covered by countless layers of late antique, medieval, Renaissance, modern, and contemporary erudition.

The sieve is also a magnifying glass: the lexica or specialized monographs guide one to the identification of the details and curiosities that are hidden in the texts of the library, and could have escaped the reader. Besides, by decontextualizing words or quotations found in books, those works of compilation produce poles of lexical coherence, or the entries of the encyclopedia of a society, whether one is dealing with fish, vegetables, or wine cups, prostitutes or jokes. The very work of Athenaeus has produced a large number of those poles of coherence, which are for us today an essential source for the reconstruction of entries concerning cuisine, nutrition, and the symposium in the encyclopedia of antiquity.

Still at the same level, where one acquires the consciousness of the mediation operated by metaliterature between the reader and the ancient library, works of erudition fulfill another function, that of the optical filters one uses on a camera in order to bring to light dimensions of reality that are not accessible to the naked eye, to modify the framing or the focus. Those filters are the various forms of technical knowledge at Athenaeus' disposal: philology, lexicography, grammar, and literary history. When they are applied to the same extract, they can bring out details, problems, and particular curiosities, as one and the same word can be part of a discussion on the constitution of the text of a verse, on spelling and accentuation norms, or on the Attic dialect. Those filters insert texts in the polyphony of interpretations and readings, but also in the chronology of second-degree reading: what does it mean to read Homer through Zenodotus or Aristarchus? And Plato through the *Against Plato's School* by Theopompus of Chios (11.508c–509b)?

Athenaeus' work, however, cannot be reduced to bibliographic itineraries and the technical observation of words and texts. Continuing upwards, one reaches the third level. To overhang the library at this level means to become conscious of a distance that is spatial and temporal at the same time, of a marked gap that inscribes the entire project of Athenaeus in the field of the archive, of conservation and recovery—in sum, to the field of cultural and linguistic archaeology. That distance does not limit itself to making books disappear, to spreading amnesia, to undoing the link between words and things; these are all effects to which the learned practices of Larensius' circle can bring a remedy, at least within some limits. It leads to the consciousness of the historicity of an entire culture through its progressive entropy, the degeneration of its practices, its ethical norms, its social values, and its behavior.

In this respect, the long treatment of the lifestyle of Homer's heroes, summarized in the first book, has the effect of suddenly recalling to memory an ideal that is no longer accessible in harmonious solidarity, in measure and simplicity.[1] That framework, moreover, constitutes a real thematic matrix for the *Deipnosophists*, since it contains all the themes that will be treated in the remainder of the work: food, wine, drinking, crowns, perfumes, incense,

---

[1] That paradigmatic value of the Homeric banquets comes back in Book 5: they represent an ideal of which the banquets of the philosophers offer but a pale reflection (5.186d ff.).

tableware, *proposis*, song, dance, games, and libations. That matrix also constitutes a point of comparison for the ulterior evolution of Greek culture. The habit of eating on couches, public baths, the excesses of refinement exhibited by cooks and perfume-makers, the very evolution of confectionery and the aphrodisiacs that come to sustain sexual activity, the music, and even the clothes and shoes, testify to the degeneration of customs, already noticed by sources of Hellenistic times (1.18b–e). In Book 14, basing himself on Aristoxenus' *Symmikta Sympotika*, Athenaeus lingers on the decadence of music, on its technical impoverishment, on the effects provoked by artists in search of the spectacular (14.631e). Corruption and barbarity have taken over the theaters, and the memory of what music of times past had been survives only by a miracle: for instance, in a feast at Poseidonia, a Greek community whose customs and language have been transformed, but which was wise enough to preserve the words and institutions of the rite. In this case, collective and festive memory has the same efficiency as the library (632a).

This temporal and historical depth is accompanied by an inevitable comparison with the social, political, linguistic, and cultural reality of the place of observation: if Larensius' banquets are the instrument of a trip through the time and space of the Greek world, they are no less rooted in the Roman world and in Latinity. The gaze directed on the library sometimes opens the way to a certain form of linguistic and cultural comparison, intent on gathering the elements of continuity or of rupture. That reference to Rome is contested by Ulpian, locked up in his "Syro-Atticist" intransigence. It is, however, present throughout the text, whether one is trying to recall to memory the existence of a Roman grammatical tradition—a distinguished practitioner of which was Varro, whom Larensius considers as his ancestor (4.160c)—or whether one is quoting a historical source on Caesar's expedition written "in the language of our fathers" (6.273b), or whether one is looking for Latin equivalents to Greek words. More subtle links appear when Roman and Attic fishmongers are compared (6.224c), or when Larensius tackles the question of slavery in Rome (6.272d–e), or when the mention of the decadence of customs in the Hellenistic world introduces a reflection on the damage provoked by lust in the Roman world (6.274c–f). Roman society also enters the space of *zētēsis*: for instance, during the reflection on the consumption of wine by women (10.440d–441a). An author like Polybius, between two worlds, plays an essential role in this. Rome and Greece come back into play at the mention of the customs related to serving wine (a task that fell on young men of noble birth: 10.425a) or the norms that regulate the consumption of pure wine (10.429a–b). Even the long list of Greeks who loved jokes extends in a totally natural way to the Latin world, where Sylla and Lucius Anicius represent the type of the *philogelōs* in its Roman version (14.615a–b). A god like Janus becomes part of the *zētēsis* concerning crowns (15.692d), and even Roman recipes find their place in Athenaeus' gourmet universe (14.647e).[2]

This meeting between two worlds, however, does not succeed in hiding the fact that the priority of the deipnosophists is the project of reconstructing a cultural and linguistic universe, that of the Greek world. At the fourth level of that helicoidal gallery that rises above the library, one does indeed reach an anthropological point of view, within which a culture reflects on itself. Finally, why did Athenaeus choose as the subject of his work the banquet, with its two successive phases of *deipnon* and *sumposion*? Why precisely this subject and not another? First of all, because the banquet makes it possible to unite the immediacy of an experienced practice—with its ritual, its codified progression, its principles of social cohabitation—with a process of cultural anamnesis that passed through conversations and searches which in turn incited one to keep drunkenness under control so as to be able to exercise intelligence. The gestures, the words, and the objects all participate in the same mnemotechnics, set under the control of Ulpian, the symposiarch and, at the same time, the guardian of the rites and the words. Secondly, because the banquet is a good "anthropological object", as one would say today. It connects the world of objects to that of cuisine, the acculturation of nature; it calls upon complex codes of civility, conviviality, complicity, and etiquette, from good table manners to the codes of the joke; it inscribes within a social framework the biological need for food. The banquet is also a place of experimentation and social control of affections and experiences, whether it is through drunkenness as a form of contact with alterity, or through erotic desire. On the other hand, the banquet lends itself to the most vast and diverse travels within the space of the library. Medicine, philosophy, cuisine, comedy, poetry, lexica, epic, epistolography, and collections of anecdotes, music, historiography, and antiquarian erudition: those different subdivisions of the ancient library are all represented in the *Deipnosophists*. Even if the members of Larensius' circle embody one or the other of those specialties, one should not forget that the one who leads the game, Athenaeus, shares, at least up to a point, their technical competence, in his capacity, for instance, to quote the authors, famous or obscure, of Hellenistic medicine, of Alexandrian erudition, or of the peripatetic tradition. Finally, as suggested by the Attic wine cups, where drinkers observed each other in the act of drinking, the banquet was always the place and time of a certain form of cultural reflection: though the music, the jokes, and the poetry that were recited there, and the subjects of

---

[2] Other noteworthy links between Greece and Rome: 14.639b–e (on Saturnalia and their Thessalian equivalent); 14.660c (on the execution of sacrifices in Rome by the highest magistrates, censors). One recognizes here Larensius' competence in matters of religion.

conversation, the sense of belonging to the same traditions was asserted, the sharing of the same universe of thought and language.

Reflexivity: every mirror presupposes maximum proximity, but also an irreducible distance, a distancing necessary to the perception of one's own image, one's own identity. Such is the position of the ethnologist or the anthropologist who studies the culture to which they belong, who must construct a point of observation that is both close and distant at the same time. That is also the position of Athenaeus before the mirror of the library: the books, and the words of the Greek language are familiar to him. However, he scans them in search of an elusive strangeness, which manifests itself in cultural codes, in ethical models, in symbolic links now all in the past and diffracted in allusions, polemics or simple literary mentions. This is true for the reflection that underlies the entire work of Athenaeus: what about food? What does it mean to eat? And how should one eat? From what point does a physiological need reveal a psychological trait, or even becomes a social deviation? Where does one place the norm of behavior and how does it happen that the transgression of the norm should carry with it a series of disorders, comical or dramatic? The contemporary reader cannot but take note of Athenaeus' inquiries and of their anthropological relevance; such inquiries, for instance, lead one to question the consumption of fish, *opsophagia*, as a paradigm of extreme gluttony: that is, to define an ethical profile and a type of social behavior, but also to introduce a form of destabilizing alterity.

Reflexivity is essential in the *Deipnosophists*: Larensius' guests renew the rite of the classical *sumposion*, and even the cooks take part in the game, showing themselves worthy imitators of the cooks of Greek comedy.[3] The gestures, the attitudes, the rules of conviviality and the progress of the meal first, and the *sumposion* after it, form the frame of the conversation, but they also define its subjects, its tone and its purpose. Telling the banquet, inventorying its phases and its variants, placing its customs within a network of information and written testimonies, whether the point is to give new life to the rules of the *kottabos*, a game of the past, or to reconstruct the art of weaving crowns from plants: those different subjects of conversation enable a gaze that is critical, distanced, and problematic for the progress and the meaning of the meeting.

Just as those literati at the banquet reflect on the banquet, so those Greek speakers reflect on their Greek language and on its conformity to the use of the ancients. But this archaeology of words, objects, dishes, and gestures leads to a more fundamental reflection, on ethical norms, on codes of life in society, on the passions, on the links between political power and power over oneself. The pleasure of eating and drinking together in the context of the *deipnon* and

---

[3] On the culinary universe of Greek comedy, see Wilkins 2000b.

the symposion is indeed put under everyone's control, tempered by the rules of conviviality and the circulation of the word, supervised by the symposiarch. And in practice, Larensius' guests do not fall into any excess that is not one of language and erudition. At the same time, however, excess is at the center of their conversation: intemperance, prodigality, lust, exaggerated gluttony, and uncontrolled propensity for wine. Those deviations enable them to satisfy specific points of curiosity, in the form of scandalous anecdotes, edifying stories, and extraordinary descriptions. They also, however, feed a reflection on the ways and the times in which a civilization sinks into excess, in which wealth becomes lust, and in which a materialistic and hedonistic society forgets its culture, its principles, and its identity.

From this particular point of view, the library demands a reflection on history: what is it that has the power to cause the decadence of a people, the fall of a city, or the crisis of a culture? A first answer immediately: all this happens at the moment when the Greeks start imitating the barbarians, let themselves be conquered by their *truphē*, and adopt their lifestyle, with its excesses of refinement. Such is the case of the Spartans, who according to Phylarchus have adopted the lifestyle of the Great King (4.141f–142b). The problem sometimes also comes from inside, and this happens when a society loosens its vigilance and lets dangerous behavior spread: Athens, Greece's *prutanaeum*, thus suffers the fury of the flatterers (6.254b). Societies that give in to *truphē* risk annihilation, as Book 12 shows with its edifying itinerary: Sybaris, Tarentum, the Iapygians, the Scythians, Miletus, which falls into civil war, the Ionians (Magnesians, Samians, Colophonians), and many other peoples. Contagion does not spare Rome. Lucullus is responsible for the introduction to Rome of the virus of *truphē* (6.274e–f), he himself having been contaminated by Mithridates, whose wealth he had acquired—and with it, his style of life (12.543a). Apicius testifies to the propagation of the disease (1.7a–d; 4.168e; 12.543b).

The banquet is also a good subject for the critique of individual customs, and the conversations of the deipnosophists develop an immense gallery of characters who are odd, extravagant, tragic, ill, ridiculous, or simply human, by virtue of weaknesses from which even the greatest among the ancients are not spared: characters emblematic of barbarian softness, Greek tyrants with extravagant tastes, effeminate Hellenistic kings obese and corroded by gout,[4] leaders escorted by prostitutes, by harpists and flute players, etc. That critique of customs offers a particular perspective for the reading of the classics, of the great authors, for entire literary genres, or even for the moral and intellectual authorities that are (or should be) the philosophers. The polyphony of

---

[4] See Gambato 2000.

the conversation makes possible the polemical diversity of points of view, but the questions nevertheless are asked: what do Plato, the Stoics, the Cyrenaics, the Peripatetics, the Epicureans, and the Cynics have to say on the evolution of customs? What answers do they provide to the questions concerning pleasure, desire, happiness, ethics, and politics? Does the example they give through their personal conduct agree with their words? What do the historians, the comic poets, and the Alexandrine grammarians have to say when those questions are addressed to them, when one applies to them a reading filter that privileges food, drink, relations with women, with youngsters, or with wine, the use of perfumes, or the choice of clothes?

Considered from that point of observation from above, but also from Rome and from its empire, the library of Greek texts, parceled out into thousands of quotations, sees the threads of its discourse pulled back together: a discourse on customs, on history, on crossings between private life and collective destinies, that is, a main concern for all those who from the Hellenistic period have attempted to understand the transformations of the world and the reversals of fortune. Athenaeus' *Deipnosophists* may reflect, beyond the erudite bulimia and the jokes of its protagonists, the anxiety of a civilization about its own future and the fragility of a cultural identity that strives to preserve its roots, its language, its authorities, and its values. This minute exploration of the world of material goods and of foods, of desires and appetites, of norms and transgressions, of measure and of excess, indubitably offers a fascinating subject of meditation to the contemporary reader. The mirror that Athenaeus turns in the direction of his culture, of his memory, of his library, and of history will not cease to invite reflection.

Works Cited

Anderson, G. 1974. "Athenaeus: The Sophistic Environment." In *Aufstieg und Niedergang der römischen Welt,* Teil II: *Principat,* Band 34.3, 2173–2185. Berlin.

———. 1993. *The Second Sophistic: A Cultural Phenomenon in the Roman Empire.* London.

———. 2000. "The Banquet of Belles-Lettres: Athenaeus and the Comic Symposium." In Braund and Wilkins 2000:116–126.

Arnott, W.G. 1996. *Alexis, the Fragments: A Commentary.* Cambridge.

———. 2000. "Athenaeus and the Epitome: Texts, Manuscripts, and Early Editions." In Braund and Wilkins 2000:41–52.

Blank, H. 1992. *Das Buch in der Antike.* Munich.

Blum, R. 1991. *Kallimachos: The Alexandrian Library and Origins of Bibliography.* Madison, WI.

Boardman, J. 1980. *The Greeks Overseas: Their Early Colonies and Trade.* New York.

Bolter, J.D. 1991. *Writing Space: The Computer, Hypertext, and the History of Writing.* Hillsdale, NJ.

Bompaire, J. 1958. *Lucien écrivain: Imitation et création.* Paris.

Boudon-Millot, V. and J. Jouanna, eds. 2010. *Galien: Ne pas se chagriner.* Vol. 4. Paris.

Bowersock, G. W. 1969. *Greek Sophists in the Roman Empire.* Oxford.

Braund, D. 2000a. "Athenaeus, 'On the Kings of Syria'." In Braund and Wilkins 2000:514–522.

———. 2000b. "Learning, Luxury, and Empire: Athenaeus' Roman Patron." In Braund and Wilkins 2000:3–22.

Braund, D. and Wilkins, J., eds. 2000. *Athenaeus and His World: Reading Greek Culture in the Roman Empire.* Exeter.

Broggiato, M. 2000. "Athenaeus, Crates, and Attic Glosses: A Problem of Attribution." In Braund and Wilkins 2000:364–371.

Callmer, C. 1944. "Antike Bibliotheken." In *Opuscula Archaeologica* 10:145–193.

Canfora, L. 1990. *The Vanished Library: A Wonder of the Ancient World.* Berkeley. [Original Italian edition: 1986. *La biblioteca scomparsa.* Palermo.]

Carruthers, M. 1990. *The Book of Memory: A Study of Memory in Medieval Culture*. Cambridge.

Champlin, E. 1980. *Fronto and Antonine Rome*. Cambridge, MA.

Cribiore, R. 2001. *Gymnastics of the Mind: Greek Education in Hellenistic and Roman Egypt*. Princeton.

Dessau, H. 1980. "Zu Athenaeus." *Hermes* 25:136–158.

Detienne, M. 1994. *The Gardens of Adonis: Spices in Greek Mythology*. Princeton.

Dorandi, T. 2000. *Le stylet et la tablette: Dans le secret des auteurs antiques*. Paris.

Dover, K.J. 1968. *Lysias and the Corpus Lysiacum*. Berkeley.

Dupont, F. 1977. *Le plaisir et la loi: Du "banquet" de Platon au "Satiricon"*. Paris.

———. 1994. *L'invention de la littérature: De l'ivresse grecque au livre latin*. Paris.

Düring, I. 1936. "De Athenaei 'Dipnosophistarum' indole atque disposition." In *Apophoreta Gotoburgensia Vilelmo Lundström oblate*, ed. H. Armini, 226–270. Göteborg.

Fedeli, P. 1998. "Biblioteche private e pubbliche a Roma e nel mondo romano." In *Le bibliotheche nel mondo antico e medievale*, ed. G. Cavallo, 31–64. Rome.

Fehrle, R. 1986. *Das Bibliothekswesen im alten Rom*. Wiesbaden.

Flemming, R. 2000. "The Physicians at the Feast: The Place of Medical Knowledge at Athenaeus' Dinner Table." In Braund and Wilkins 2000:476–482.

Fraser, P.M. 1972. *Ptolemaic Alexandria*. 3 vols. Oxford.

Frazier, F. and J. Sirinelli, eds. 1996. *Plutarque: Propos de Table, Livres VII-IX (Moralia* vol. 9). Paris.

Gambato, M. 2000. "The Female-Kings: Some Aspects of the Representation of Eastern Kings in Athenaeus' *Deipnosophistae*." In Braund and Wilkins 2000:227–230.

Grant, M. 2000. *Galen on Food and Diet*. London.

Helmbold, W.C. and E.N. O'Neil. 1959. *Plutarch's Quotations*. Baltimore.

van den Hoek, A. 1996. "Techniques of Quotation in Clement of Alexandria: A View of Ancient Literary Working Methods." In *Vigiliae Christianae* 50:223–243.

Jacob, C. 2000. "Athenaeus the Librarian." In Braund and Wilkins 2000:85–110.

Jeanneret, M. 1986. *Des mets et des mots: Banquets et propos de table à la Renaissance*. Paris.

Kaibel, G., ed. 1887–1890. *Athenaei Naucratitae Deipnosophistarum Libri XV*. 3 vols. Leipzig.

Lallot, J., ed. 1998. *La grammaire de Denys le Thrace*. 2nd ed. Paris

Langie, A. 1908. *Les bibliothèques publiques dans l'ancienne Rome et dans l'Empire romain*. Fribourg.

Lissarague, F. 1987. *Un flot d'images: Une esthétique du banquet grec*. Paris.

Lukinovich, A. 1990. "The Play of Reflections between Literary Form and the Sympotic Theme in the *Deipnosophistae* of Athenaeus." In *Sympotica: A Symposium on the "Symposion"*, ed. O. Murray, 263–271. Oxford.

Martin, J. 1931. *Symposion: Die Geschichte einer literarischen Form*. Paderborn.

Mengis, K. 1920. *Die schriftstellerische Technik im Sophistenmahl des Athenaios*. Paderborn.

Moeller, A. 2000. *Naucratis: Trade in Archaic Greece*. Oxford.

Olson, S. Douglas and A. Sens, eds. *Archestratos of Gela: Greek Culture and Cuisine in the Fourth Century BC*. Oxford.

Olson, S. Douglas. 2007-2012. *Athenaeus: The Learned Banqueters*. 8 vols. Loeb Classical Library. Cambridge, MA.

Pelling, C. 2000. "Fun with Fragments: Athenaeus and the Historians." In Braund and Wilkins 2000:171–190.

Pernot, L. 1993. *La rhétorique de l'éloge dans le monde gréco-romain*. 2 vols. Paris.

Pesando, F. 1994. *Libri e biblioteche*. Roma.

Relihan, J.C. 1992. "Rethinking the History of the Literary Symposium." *Illinois Classical Studies* 17:213–244.

Rodrigues-Noriega Guillén, L. 2000. "Are the Fifteen Books of the *Deipnosophistae* an Excerpt?" In Braund and Wilkins 2000:244–255.

Romeri, L. 2000. "The *logodeipnon*: Athenaeus between Banquet and Anti-banquet." In Braund and Wilkins 2000:256–271.

Schmitt-Pantel, P. 1992. *La cité au banquet: Histoire des repas publics dans les cités grecques*. Rome.

Schmitz, T. 1997. *Bildung und Macht: Zur sozialen und politischen Funktion der zweiten Sophistik in der greichischen Welt der Kaiserzeit*. Munich.

Skydsgaard, J.E. 1968. *Varro the Scholar: Studies in the First Book of Varro's "De re rustica."* Hafniae.

Slater, W.J. 1982. "Aristophanes of Byzantium and Problem Solving in the Museum." *Classical Quarterly* 32:330–349.

Small, J.P. 1997. *Wax Tablets of the Mind: Cognitive Studies of Memory and Literacy in Classical Antiquity*. London.

Swain, S. 1996. *Hellenism and Empire: Language, Classicism, and Power in the Greek World, AD 50-250*. Oxford.

Thompson, D. 2000. "Athenaeus in his Egyptian Context." In Braund and Wilkins 2000:77–84.

Too, Y.L. 2000. "The Walking Library. The Performances of Cultural Memories." In Braund and Wilkins 2000:111–123.

———. 2010. *The Idea of the Library in the Ancient World*. Oxford.

Trapp, M. 2000. "Plato in the *Deipnosophistae*." In Braund and Wilkins 2000:353–363.

Wendel, C. 1955. "Das griechische-römische Altertum." In *Handbuch der Bibliothekwissenschaft*, ed. F. Milkau and G. Leyh, 3/1.2. Wiesbaden.

Whitmarsh, T. 2000. "The Politics and Poetics of Parasitism: Athenaeus on Parasites and Flatterers." In Braund and Wilkins 2000:304–315.

Wilkins, J. 2000a. "Athenaeus and the 'Fishes' of Archippus." In Braund and Wilkins 2000:523–535.

———. 2000b. *The Boastful Chef: The Discourse of Food in Ancient Greek Comedy.* Oxford.

———. 2000c. "Dialogue and Comedy: The Structure of the *Deipnosophistae*." In Braund and Wilkins 2000:23–37.

Zecchini, G. 1989. *La cultura storica di Ateneo*. Milan.

Index

Lysanias, 99
Lysias, 64, 67
Lysimachus, 68

Macrobius, ix, 14
Magnes, 63n24
Magnus (symposiast in
  Deipnosophists), 26, 75
Man who Loved the Pipes (Philetairus),
  43
Marcianus A (Codex Marcianus 447),
  9, 35, 100n6
Marcus Aurelius (Roman emperor),
  20, 23, 58
Marius, 20
Marriage of Ceyx (Hesiod), 67, 88
The Master of Debaucheries (Alexis), 67
Masurius (symposiast in
  Deipnosophists), 24, 25, 26, 43, 49,
  79
Matron the Parodist, 59
Melampus, 106
memory, memorization, and
  mnemotechnics, 75–80, 101
Menander, 51, 63n24, 92
Menedemus, 81n14
Mengis, K., 44n5
Menodotus, 59
menus, 41–42
Metagenes, 53
metaliterature, 114–115
Midas, 106
Minos (Antiphanes), 72
Miscellaneous Notes (Aristoxenus),
  102n9
Mithridates, 119
Mnemosyne (goddess), 42
Mnesimachus, 64
Moesia: Larensius as procurator of,
  21, 90
Monarchy (Theophrastus), 67
Moral Letters to Lucilius (Seneca), 79n9
Moschion, 59

mullet, 53
mūma, 43, 49, 90n3
Museum of Alexandria, viii, ix, x,
  21–22, 26, 31, 56–57, 82–83
music and musicians, ix, 16, 19, 26, 33,
  36, 42–43, 72, 85, 90, 105, 116, 117
Myrtilus (symposiast in
  Deipnosophists): dialogue of, 50,
  51, 52, 53; library of, 58; memory
  of, 78; as pornographer, 39, 58;
  as reader, 73; role of Ulpian and
  Cynulcus in structure of text
  and, 38, 39; slave of, 76; web of
  connections, game of weaving,
  105; on women, 39, 50; on words
  and language, 91, 92

Natural History (Pliny the Elder), 79n8
Naucratis (Egypt), 9–10, 11, 60, 62
Neaera (Philemon), 50
Neleus of Scepsis, 22
Nero (Roman emperor), 56n7
Nestor's cup, 101n7
Nicander of Colophon, 2, 50, 72, 76, 89
Nicander of Thyateira, 87
Nicholas of Damascus, 61n20, 62–63
Nicochares, 1
Nicostratus of Cyprus, 55
Noctes Atticae (*Attic Nights*; Aulus
  Gellius), ix, 55n2, 58–59, 74n3,
  102n10
normativity, linguistic, 86, 90–94
Notes (Hegesander of Delphi), 91
novelty: of conversations in
  Deipnosophists (Athenaeus), 103,
  106–107; poikilia, concept of, 47,
  48, 100, 103, 109
Numa Pompilius, 20

Odyssey, 25, 59, 81n14
oikoumenē, *Deipnosophists* as epitome
  or synthesis of, 109–12
Olympians (Pindar), 64

Lightning Source UK Ltd.
Milton Keynes UK
UKHW021118070221
378324UK00009B/368

9 780674 073289